The Re[illegible]

Cookbook

III Edition

Stephanie Kenrose

ISBN 978-0578099088

Contents

Foreward to the Third Edition

When I wrote the first Reactive Hypoglycemia Cookbook with the intent to help people who - like me - were suffering from what can be a debilitating disease, I certainly never expected such a runaway success. Every day I received dozens of letters from readers who this book has helped. I also receive many suggestions, some of which I have incorporated into this, the third edition of the book. Included in this edition are suggestions for substituting meat and meat substitutes in the recipes, to please everyone from vegans to meat eaters. There are plenty of vegetarian options, some of which will appeal to meat eaters (you'll be surprised about how meaty a portabella mushroom tastes!). Why the emphasis on vegetables? As you'll find out from the accompanying chapters, vegetarians and vegans simply fare much better with blood sugar issues than their meat eating counterparts. That said, if you eat meat - you won't be deprived. There are plenty of dishes which include meat options.

Please continue to send your letters - it's a good feeling to know so many people are being helped by such a simple cookbook.

Good luck with your reactive hypoglycemia journey!

Stephanie Kenrose

What is Reactive Hypoglycemia?

Reactive hypoglycemia, also known as Postprandial Reactive Hypoglycemia (PRH) in the medical establishment, is a term used to describe the hypoglycemia that occurs 2 to 4 hours after a meal (usually, a meal high in carbohydrates).

Postprandial = symptoms occur after meals (post "after" + Latin prandium "luncheon")
Reactive = symptoms that occur as a response to food intake
Hypoglycemia = low blood sugar

Simply put, reactive hypoglycemia happens like this: you consume a meal that is typically high in carbs and simple sugars, say, a Big Mac, fries and a Coke or a turkey sandwich on white bread, potato chips and a cola. Your body "freaks out" at the high sugar load now existing in your blood from all this high-carb food and your pancreas produces too much insulin to compensate and bring your blood sugar down. So much insulin, in fact, that the other blood sugar regulators—glucagon and epinephrine—can't cope with the high sugar load in your bloodstream. The result from this imbalance is reactive hypoglycemia—low blood sugar—which causes you to become irritable and lethargic. If you don't act on your body's signal that you need to eat something, you might get shakes, shivers, chills, and heart palpitations at around the 3 hour mark after eating, or if the Twinkie defense is to be believed, you might become aggressive, violent, or exhibit other kinds of personality disorders (now you know why you told your boss he's an ass at that 11:00 a.m. meeting).

In experiments on rodents, alcohol and oral glucose combined was shown to trigger reactive hypoglycemia. When combined with stress, the reactive hypoglycemia response worsened

Of course, not all reactive hypoglycemics respond to their low blood sugar by buying a gun and shooting the San Francisco Supervisor, but many of us are plagued by an elusive condition that can cause symptoms of stress, depression, mood swings, and PMS-like symptoms.

At first, researchers thought reactive hypoglycemia was connected to diabetes; while diabetics suffer from too little insulin, reactive hypoglycemic exhibit symptoms which seem to suggest they have too much insulin (in fact, when I describe what I have to friends, I often find myself saying I have the opposite of diabetes). The symptoms that reactive hypoglycemics experience with food-induced low blood sugar are indistinguishable from a diabetic experiencing insulin-induced low blood sugar. Simply put, when reactive hypoglycemics eat a carb-heavy meal, they experience an unpleasant reaction usually around 2 hours after the meal, as their blood sugar drops.

Symptoms

Symptoms can be numerous and varied, and include:

- Anxiety
- Apathy
- Belligerence
- Blurred vision
- Depression
- Difficulty in thinking
- Dizziness
- Faintness
- Feeling unable to perform complex tasks, like driving
- Hunger
- Irritability
- Lethargy
- Nightmares
- Palpitations

- Personality change
- Rage
- Seizures
- Sleeplessness
- Slurred speech
- Stomach upsets
- Sweating
- Tingling
- Tremors
- Un-coordination (appearing drunk)
- Weakness

You may have just some of the above symptoms. Rarely, reactive hypoglycemia will present itself as an odd set of symptoms that seemingly has no relation to hypoglycemia, or any of the more common symptoms listed above. For instance, in one study, an arthritic patient reported experiencing pain in his hip after sugary meals. Switching to a low carb diet decreased the patient's pain significantly (Lev-Ran, A. & Anderson, R. (1981)

The key is figuring out if your symptoms are occurring after a meal, and if the symptoms are being caused by low blood sugar. One way to determine this is to keep a food diary, noting when your symptoms are occurring. If your symptoms tend to occur 2 to 4 hours after you ingest high carbs (including alcohol, French fries, baked potatoes, chips, white bread, white pasta, and sodas) it may be time for further diagnostic tools like a Home Glucose Test to determine your blood sugar levels at the time of the symptoms.

Diet

Not surprisingly, a poor diet is a contributing factor to reactive hypoglycemia. Well-conducted studies on this subject are lacking, but some studies indicate that a low fat, high carb diet contributes to reactive hypoglycemia.[i] Internist Richard Podell[ii] states that 40% of his patients with sugar-related problems improve after they start an anti-hypoglycemic diet: one that is free of simple carbs like white bread and pasta, and is sugar, caffeine and alcohol restricted. Also, people on a calorie restricted diet may also be at risk, especially when eating primarily high-carb foods. Other factors that may contribute to the disease include alcohol (one experiment showed that the equivalent of three gin and tonics can cause reactive hypoglycemia[iii]) and there is also a possibility that a calcium deficiency in the diet may be a cause.[iv]

Diet as a Treatment Option

In one study in the mid-1980s, researchers gave eight subjects suspected of having reactive hypoglycemia a euglycemic (blood sugar friendly) diet. Symptoms (including depression) disappeared on the euglycemic diet, but when the subjects returned to their previous junk food diets, all experienced reactive hypoglycemia again. The researchers concluded that a diet free of refined sugar and caffeine helps alleviate depression, anxiety, and fatigue in people with reactive hypoglycemia.[v]

However, this was a tiny study; if only it were as easy as not drinking coffee and avoiding sugar! Everyone's body is different, and finding the right diet for reactive hypoglycemia can be frustrating. There is no "magic diet," it's really a case of trial and error. All diets for reactive hypoglycemia recommend the elimination of caffeine and sugars (fructose is okay in some), the reduction of refined carbs, and state that that those vegetables with a low glycemic index can be eaten often. Supplements like flax seed, nutritional yeast flakes, vitamins, calcium supplements, lipoic acid, *Gymnema sylvestre,* 5-HTTP, St. John's Wort, and garlic have been proposed by some to ameliorate the symptoms of reactive hypoglycemia,[vi] and they certainly can't hurt.

The glycemic index ranks carbohydrates according to their effect on blood sugar levels. Although the glycemic index can be helpful in sorting out which foods to avoid and which to favor, it shouldn't be relied upon as the only source of information about diet.

The diet recommended by Seale Harris was the elimination of all fresh fruits, whole grains, and legumes with the majority of calories coming from fatty animal products. Later diets (including the Atkins) built upon this and encouraged a high-protein, low-carb intake (including the reduction of starchy vegetables and fruit), mega doses of vitamins. In addition, there were a few quirky diets that recommended receiving full spectrum light, avoiding microwave ovens, and only eating raw milk and fertile eggs.

The Paavo Airola diet is low in animal products and high in whole grains, nuts seeds, legumes, vegetables and fruit.[vii] It is this diet that worked for me, so most of this book is based around that premise.

Whatever diet you choose, a low-carb diet and frequent small split meals should be the first treatment for reactive hypoglycemia.[viii] Adding two small meals, one mid-morning and one mid-afternoon, should be the first step.[ix] I also found that eating a slice of "Ezekiel 4:9" bread with two tablespoons of peanut butter immediately before bed helps my blood glucose stabilize overnight. I've tried various other foods: handfuls of peanuts, a low-carb, high-protein snack bar, high-protein, low carb raisin-bread, but nothing works for me like the Ezekiel 4:9 no-wheat bread. A high-fiber, restricted-simple sugar diet full of fruits and vegetables is a must. In other words, skip the Big Mac and have a Southwestern Salad instead. Load on all the veggies at Subway, choose the whole wheat bread and skip the chips and soda (yes, even the baked chips). Here are some tips to follow when creating your new diet:

Tip #1: Eat Carbohydrates

Your body needs carbs to regulate blood sugar. You may have already encountered some websites that recommend things like "55% of energy as carbohydrate" in a diet or "try a low carb, high protein diet" or "less than x grams of simple carbohydrate daily." The true answer is to eat a balanced diet, and monitor your blood sugar closely

Tip #2: Swap white bread and noodles for whole grains.

There's no doubt about it, there are going to be those times you don't feel like cooking, and you reach for something simple, like a sandwich or a burger in a bun. That's why it's important to replace the products you normally buy with their whole grain alternatives (when I reach in freezer and grab a whole wheat bun and a bean burger, it's impossible to feel guilt!). Complex carbohydrates like whole grain crackers, bagels, and cereal deliver glucose over a longer period of time, resulting in a slower sugar response.

Tip #3: Choose cereals carefully

Shop in a health food store if you can, as you are more likely to find "hidden" ingredients in cereal like High Fructose Corn Syrup or Sugar. Did you know that the first ingredient in Apple Jacks is sugar? I only found that out after my son, Leo (who also has hereditary reactive hypoglycemia), consumed a large bowl and hours later was in a bad mood thanks to a blood sugar drop. I look for low-carb, no sugar cereals like

Kamut Flakes or Kashi Whole Grain Puffs. Ezekiel 4:9 bread is Low GI, and full of protein. We use that instead of regular bread, but you can try another (no sugar) whole grain product.

Tip #4: Drink water or non-caffeinated tea instead of soda

There is some research to suggest that some artificial sweeteners may produce an insulin response,[x] so they are best avoided, especially considering many soft drinks also contain caffeine! Buy sparkling water or lime-flavored sparkling water. I've tried just about every herbal tea in the book, and I settled on one that actually tasted good, like hot lemonade (Lemon Mate). You *may* be able to tolerate caffeine; I learned to restrict coffee to one, very small cup in the morning. Any more than that precipitates a blood sugar crash for me.

Tip #5: Eat every two hours

Only you can determine how often you need to eat (that's why it's a good idea to check your blood sugar using a home blood glucose monitoring device and make sure you eat before your blood sugar gets a chance to dip below 70 mg/dL), but the two hour rule works for most people to avoid a crash. That equates to about eight meals a day, starting at 8 a.m. and finishing at 10 p.m. It's important to take the portion of food that you would normally eat for a meal, and split it into two (or one third and two thirds).

For example, I eat the cereal at 8 and the toast at 10. I do the same for lunch, and divide what I would normally eat into two meals (i.e. I eat the sandwich and fruit at noon and the soup at 2).

Tip #6: Read Your Labels

I shop at a local health food store, because I became so frustrated at buying products at local grocery stores. Food manufacturers sneak sugar and High Fructose Corn Syrup into everything! For example, I bought home two jars of Planter's Dry Roasted Peanuts, and was dismayed to find out later on that they put sugar on them as a coating. Even small amounts of sugar spike my blood sugar and cause a crash so I absolutely have to avoid it if I am to maintain and even blood sugar level! I had a similar problem buying yoghurt, bread, and just about every product you can think of. Organic products and vegan products (i.e. soy yoghurt instead of regular) tend to be sweetened with evaporated cane syrup, which does not cause blood sugar spikes like sugar and high fructose corn syrup.

Tip #7: Learn to Love Fruit and Veggies

It took some getting used to, but we purged our cupboards of snack foods except for whole grain crackers, vegan cream cheese, and fruits/veggies. We eat stir fries, soups, salads, vegan chili, and other dishes bursting with vegetables. A diet rich in fruits and vegetables is a must to maintain blood sugar levels.

Tip #8: Drink and Eat Before You Exercise

Exercise lowers your blood sugar, which is great for diabetics, but not so great for the reactive hypoglycemic. I have to drink fruit juice and eat half an energy bar before I exercise, and fruit juice plus the other half of the bar afterward, otherwise I cannot exercise without feeling sick.

Tip #9: What to do if Your Blood Sugar Drops

When blood glucose drops, high carb foods can bring it back up to normal; at the first sign of low blood sugar (shakes, sweaty hands, churning stomach or another symptom which may be specific to you), you *must* eat a meal or a snack. Diabetics will often consume sugar, candy, or soda to raise blood sugar quickly. This is a *bad idea* for reactive hypoglycemics and is unnecessary. If you learn to eat at the first sign of symptoms, you will ward off a hypoglycemic attack. In an emergency, choose glucose tablets (available in the diabetic section of your local pharmacy) followed by nuts or a wholegrain bagel, or fruit juice over candy or cola, which will quickly spike your blood sugar and encourage it to fall rapidly.

Tip #10: Carry a Snack Everywhere You Go

Packs of nuts, a piece of fruit, or a healthy drink (i.e. a small carton of apple juice). Carry something so that at the first sign of something amiss…you have something to eat.

Tip #11: Keep a Jar of Pectin or Guar Gum in Your Cupboard and Use it as a Food Additive.

Pectin (a fiber found in apples, citrus fruits, grapes, berries, and bran) and guar (used as a thickening agent in many products like yoghurt and sauces) have been shown to improve reactive hypoglycemia.[xi]

Tip #12: Keep a Food Diary

Keeping a food diary can be the first step toward controlling your reactive hypoglycemia. If you see a dietician, make sure you take your notes with you, so that the dietician can better design a diet for you. There are so many causes for reactive hypoglycemia; there is no "miracle diet" that will work for everyone. It took me a month of trial and error to find a balance for my condition. I noted which foods caused my blood sugar to crash and I avoided them completely, eating only those things I knew for certain would not cause my symptoms to appear. I went on a severely carb and calorie restricted diet (I was desperate to stop my symptoms). This meant that for the first month, my family wasn't too fussed about being served soup and salad for dinner, every night. We had plenty of "variation": lentil soup and Caesar salad, vegetable soup and garden salad, minestrone (whole wheat macaroni) and Mandarin orange salad. And yes, it was boring, but worth it because I didn't get sick! Lunches and breakfasts were made from a few basic ingredients: Quorn (a chicken substitute), vegetables and fruits, wholegrain products, Vegenaise, and a handful of no-sugar, unrefined, no animal-product items.

Reference

Lev-Ran A, Anderson RW. The diagnosis of postprandial hypoglycemia. *Diabetes,* 1981, *30,* 996-999.

Sample Diets and Suggested Foods

The following sample diet is an example of what I ate for the first month. There was very little variation on this. I chose different breakfast cereals from the suggested foods list, substituting it on some days for the toast. Each day was a different soup and salad, and I swapped out the Quorn & Chicken stir fry for other vegetable and nutrient rich dishes. This sample diet has no sugar, is high in fiber and nutrients, low fat, and is low on the glycemic index.

Sample Diet for the first month

Breakfast (8 a.m.)

1 slice of Ezekiel 4:9 plain toast with buttery spread

1 cup homemade, no-sugar pinto beans

Mid-morning snack (10 a.m.)

1 piece of low-sugar fruit (i.e. apple or greenish banana)

Lunch (noon)

Quorn Chik'n stir fry (Quorn, veggies, canola oil, a few spices)

Afternoon snack (2 p.m.)

1 cup apple juice

4 small wholegrain crackers

Second Afternoon snack (4 p.m.)

Handful of carrots with 4T hummus

Dinner (6 p.m.)

1 cup of homemade soup

1 cup of salad

Because this diet tightly controlled my blood sugar by restricting carbs in the latter half of the day, I could make it through the night without eating. I had to be militant about following it. Otherwise, I would be hungry in the evenings or worse, I would experience blood sugar lows any time I skipped a meal or snack.

I added free range eggs after a couple of weeks and started making omelets (soy milk, salt & pepper, fresh veggies and vegan cheese). Adding one or two ingredients a day, I figured out a reasonable diet plan for me and my son. He's a little luckier, and he can still eat my favorite snack food without symptoms: salt and vinegar potato chips. Alas, I cannot. Here is a typical day's food for me now; this may not work for you. For example, I can tolerate a small cup of half-caffeinated coffee, but caffeine can wreak havoc on a reactive hypoglycemic, so that's why it's so important to keep a food diary:

Sample Diet after One Month

Breakfast (8 a.m.)

Small cup of ½ caffeinated, ½ decaffeinated coffee

1 slice of Ezekiel 4:9 raisin toast with butter

1 piece of fruit

Mid-morning snack (10 a.m.)

1 cup Kamut flakes

½ cup soy milk

Lunch (noon)

Stir fried vegetables, brown rice (¼ cup) and beans

Afternoon snack (2 p.m.)

1 organic, live food bar

1 cup apple juice

Late afternoon snack (4 p.m.)

Handful of carrots and hummus

Dinner (6 p.m.)

1 cup chili

Handful of wholegrain, baked tortilla chips

Evening snack (8 p.m.)

1 cup frozen fruit

Bedtime (10 p.m.)

1 slice of Ezekiel 4:9 toast with peanut butter

I don't stick rigidly to the amount of food, although I do stick to the timing. If I miss a two-hour meal I'll sometimes get grumpy and lightheaded. I get hungry; I'll eat a banana or a small bowl of baked, whole-grain tortilla chips and salsa. I also take a multivitamin and a calcium supplement to make sure my symptoms aren't caused by a lack of calcium or fuddled by a vitamin deficiency.

I avoid any artificial sugars, but you may find them palatable. Personally, I prefer fructose, a type of sugar that does not raise my blood sugar (and therefore I do not experience a big drop). Fructose is typically 60% sweeter than regular sugar, so you can add less to recipes, like oatmeal cookies. That doesn't necessarily make it healthy—it's still a sugar, and not everyone will be able to tolerate it. I found both fructose and evaporated cane syrup (which I can also tolerate in small quantities) in my local health food store, and I have also been experimenting with xylitol, a natural sugar that also does not raise my blood sugar. I tried it in a stir fry recipe (replacing the brown sugar with it), and my whole family loved it! Xylitol can be found in your local health food store.

A List of Possible Foods

This list is comprised of products that should not cause you to have a hypoglycemic reaction. The foods in bold tend to be lower on the Glycemic Index (GI) and should be tolerated by everyone. Other foods listed are higher in the Glycemic Index; if you consume these be sure to balance your meal. For example, if you eat a ripe banana (high GI), balance it with a handful of nuts (high fat). Foods marked with an asterisk can be found in any health food store. You may differ in the foods that cause your blood sugar to elevate: keep a food diary to figure out your sensitivities, and don't eat multiple foods at once before you know for sure which ingredients you can tolerate well. For example, instead of having soup and salad for lunch, have the soup at noon and the salad at 2 p.m. Splitting up foods like this will allow you to figure out what foods raise and crash your blood sugar, and which do not.

A note on serving sizes: I stuck to the serving sizes indicated on products during the first month. For example, Amy's soup has 2 servings in a can. One serving equals one meal. If I was still hungry, I would eat a garden salad to fill me up (with one serving of salad dressing). I also began to buy almost exclusively organic products, because "regular" manufacturers have a nasty habit of sneaking in sugar and other unwanted substances into products. For example, I found sugar as an ingredient in Planter's dry roasted peanuts, sugar in Jif peanut butter, sugar and/or high fructose corn syrup in most supermarket whole wheat bread (including whole grain bread!), and the list goes on. Organic manufacturers seem to pride themselves in not

Evaporated cane juice does not undergo the same refining process as regular sugar, and retains most of its nutrients and vitamins.

using sugar or high fructose corn syrup; I also got entirely bored of reading labels and looking up those alien sounding substances to figure out if I could eat them or not!

I included even innocuous sounding ingredients like baking powder. It was important for me to know *every ingredient* that was going into my body, because I thought it could be just that one small serving of an innocuous sounding ingredient that was setting me off. It turns out I was right: I cannot eat white bread products that contain evaporated cane juice. However, I can tolerate evaporated cane juice in just about every other product. My best guess is that the carb load for white bread and cane juice is just too high, and that my body needs to stay under a certain threshold.

Bold foods should be tolerated by all.
Asterisked * foods are available in health food stores.

All-Bran
Apple juice, no sugar added
Apples
Arrowhead Mills Graham Cracker Crust
Arrowhead Mills Kamut Flakes*
Baking powder
Balsamic vinegar
Bananas (ripe)
Bananas (slightly green)
Barley
Barley flakes
Bean Burgers (no bun)

Beans, dried and/or canned
Beets
Bob's Red Mill baking products*
Bran
Bread, Ezekiel 4:9
Bread, pumpernickel
Bread, sourdough
Breakfast cereal, organic, sweetened with evaporated cane juice or fruit juice*
Brown rice
Buckwheat groats*
Bulgur
Cappuccino (soy, decaf)
Carrots
Cheese, soy or rice products (no dairy)
Cherries
Chick peas
Chocolate chip cookies, vegan, sweetened with evaporated cane juice*
Citric acid
Coffee (half caf)
Coffee creamer, Silk (soy)
Corn tortillas
Cornstarch
Cream cheese, vegan, (try Tofutti brand)
Dill pickle
Dill relish (no sugar added)
Dressing, Amy's Gingerly Dressing
Dressing: Newman's Own Raspberry Vinaigrette
Dried Apricots
Edamame
Eggs (I only buy free range eggs)
Energy bars, raw food (i.e. WildBar)*

Flaxseed*
Flour, whole wheat
Fructose*
Fruit roll ups, 100% fruit, organic
Garden Salad
Garlic
Grapefruit
Grapefruit juice
Grapes
Green peas
Guacamole
Hamburger buns, Ezekiel 4:9
Herbs
Hot dogs, vegetarian, whole-wheat bun
Hummus
Indian curry
Jalapenos
Jelly, 100% fruit
Kashi 7-grain cereal puffs
Kavli crispy thin crackers*
Kiwi
Lentils
Mango
Miso soup
Morningstar Farms products (i.e. bean burgers, meatless crumbles)
Mustard
Nayonaise*
Nutritional yeast flakes
Nuts (plain or raw)
Oatmeal
Oils (I stick with olive oil mostly, sometimes canola and peanut for flavor)
Olives

Oranges
Peach
Peaches
Peanut butter
Pear
Pineapple juice
Plum
Plums
Quinoa
Quorn Chik'n Cutlets, unbreaded
Quorn nuggets, unbreaded,
Quorn products
Raw food bars*
Rolled oats
Roti (an Indian bread)
Ryvita dark rye crackers*
Salsa, organic
Salt
Sesame seeds
Soup, Amy's, all varieties
Sour Cream, vegan
Soy milk, sweetened with evaporated cane juice
Soy milk, unsweetened
Soy sauce
Soy yoghurt (sweetened with fructose or evaporated cane syrup)
Soybeans
Spaghetti & lasagna noodles, whole grain
Spaghetti Sauce, organic
Spices
Spread, vegan buttery
Strawberries

Sunflower seeds
Sushi (vegetable, 6 pieces)
Sweet potato fries
Sweet corn
Tabouli
Tahini
Tea, caffeinated
Tea, Herbal & decaffeinated
Tofu, any variety
Tofu, plain
Tofurkey sandwich slices
Tofutti ice cream
Tomato
Tomato juice and tomato sauce, organic
Tortilla, sprouted grain*
Vanilla extract
Vegenaise*
White potatoes in very small amounts (i.e. in soups)
White wine
Whole grain bagels and bread (without added sugar)
Wild rice
Xanitol*
Yam
Yeast

Food to Avoid

This list would not be complete without stating which foods should not be consumed. These are the most likely suspects that will raise your blood sugar faster than you can say High Fructose Corn Syrup. When I first starting purging my cupboards of anything that might be contributing to my reactive hypoglycemia, one of the first items to go was indeed, High Fructose Corn Syrup (HFCS). Americans consume more HFCS—an often genetically modified, cheap to produce product that has been linked to a host of disorders including diabetes—than real sugar. After reading about the complicated chemical process that is required to make HFCS, and how every dietician recommends that anyone with a blood sugar disorder should avoid HFCS, I set about purging my cupboards of the substance. Heinz Ketchup. Pancake Syrup. Black Bean Soup: some of our favorite products just had to go. We switched the pancake syrup for real berries, and the Black Bean Soup for Amy's organic soups. We use HP sauce (a British steak sauce you can find in places like World Market) in place of ketchup.

I was dismayed to find that we had to completely change our diet. I had considered myself health conscious and used to purchase whole wheat and whole grain bread: you would rarely find a loaf of white in my cupboard. I knew white bread was a no-no for health, but whole grain bread sweetened with HFCS? Who would have thought? Here is a list of the top items I no longer consume.

Top Ten Foods to Avoid

Supermarket bread products: white bread, bagels, pizza, burger buns, or other "white" bread products. During the refining process, nearly all of the fiber and nutrients are lost.[xii] Substitute whole grain products instead.

White spaghetti noodles: substitute whole grain products. Be careful to find "whole grain" and not whole wheat.

Most breakfast cereals. Apple Jacks was one of my son's favorite cereals until we read the label and discovered its #1 ingredient is sugar. Most cereals we find are completely unpalatable and cause a blood sugar reaction a couple of hours later. I can eat Arrowhead Mills Kamut Flakes, Oatmeal, All-Bran, and Kashi 7-grain cereal. Leo can eat a wider variety, but all come from the health food store and none have sugar or HFCS. He recently found a box of corn flakes sweetened with fruit juice that he loved.

Anything that has "sugar" or "high fructose corn syrup" as an ingredient. This sounds simple, but it really isn't. You'd be surprised at where you find sugar: packaged meals, soups, canned beans, yoghurts, ice-cream, fruit cups, and baked goods. I stopped shopping at my local grocery store because of this problem. If I do go there, I stick to the produce aisle and the green or vegan section.
Sodas and fruit juices. The exception to this are tiny, one serving boxes of apple juice. I used to drink a wide variety of things, but now my list has diminished to a few products: water, coffee (one tiny cup in the morning), tea (mostly herbal) and apple juice on occasion. Anything else causes problems. I don't even drink diet drinks: they can have

hidden caffeine, and I can't always trust myself to remember to check labels.

Pastries, muffins, cakes, and other "treats": There are a few treats I can have, including vegan chocolate chip cookies from my local health food stores. Why vegan? Chocolate chips in regular cookies are usually made with sugar: vegan cookies are usually made with honey, fructose, or evaporated cane sugar (which is as close to the plant as you can get). Those products I can tolerate in small amounts.

Restaurant meals: I avoid eating anything in a restaurant unless I am 100% certain that sugar is not one of the ingredients. This is such a problem that we rarely eat at restaurants anymore! There are exceptions: Indian food never causes me a problem (Indians tend not to add sugar to their meals), Sweet Tomatoes/Soup Plantation (you can't beat a salad buffet), most items in Greek restaurants (except white pita) and vegetable fajitas at our local Mexican restaurant (I skip the tortillas and use corn chips instead). I can also eat tortilla chips and salsa in seemingly unlimited quantities. Not so good for me but so delicious!

White potatoes, including baked potatoes and fries: except in small amounts, in a soup for example. I completely gave up trying to have these in my diet. They are just too high in sugars for me to be able to tolerate them: I substitute a small portion of sweet potato fries, and sometimes make sweet potato chili fries.

High fat meats: when I first tried to control my reactive hypoglycemia, I went on a strict vegan diet. I had read about the benefits of such a diet, and it worked wonders for me. I am now vegetarian, and substitute low-calorie, nutrient dense products like Quorn, vegan burger crumbles, tofu, bean burgers, Tofurkey, and other meat analogues.

Potato chips and tortilla chips. Leo can eat potato chips; I cannot. We can both eat tortilla chips, but that bad habit (full of carbs and not much else) may catch up to us someday. Instead, we substitute baked, whole grain tortilla chips (available at most grocery stores in the health food section).

Recipes

A Note on Nutrition Facts

Percent daily values in recipes are based on the Reference Daily Intake (RDI) for a 2000 calorie diet.

Easy Snack Suggestions

You'll need to eat plenty of snacks during the course of the day (I eat every two hours to maintain my blood sugar level). Aim for plenty of variety. Choose one of the healthful snacks listed here for each snack.

- ¼ cup no-sugar added trail mix
- ¼ cup sunflower seeds
- 2oz cashews
- Nature's Choice multigrain cereal bars
- 6ea Triscuit whole grain crackers topped with thinly sliced cheese
- 1 cup sliced cucumbers and tomatoes with 1 Tbsp mustard sauce (see sauce recipe for Egg and Tomato fans)
- ½ Wild Bar raw food bar
- ½ cup carrots with 2 Tbsp hummus
- 2oz peanuts
- 6ea Brazil nuts
- ½ can Amy's soup
- 1 slice whole grain or sprouted grain bread with 1Tbsp peanut butter
- 1ea apple
- 1ea pear
- 1ea plum
- 1 cup cherries
- 1ea grapefruit
- 1 cup decaf cappuccino or latte with soy milk
- 1ea orange, tangerine, or mandarin orange
- 1ea peach
- 1ea hardboiled egg

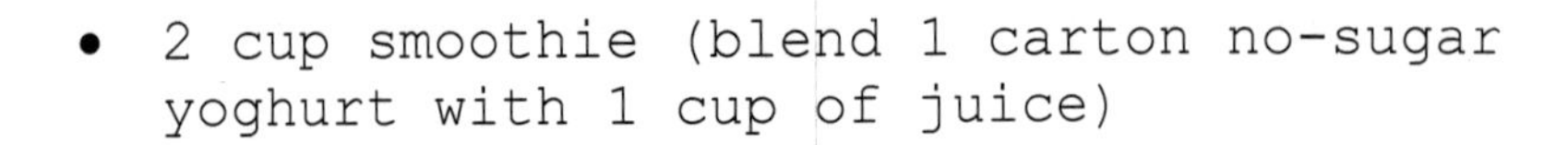

- 2 cup smoothie (blend 1 carton no-sugar yoghurt with 1 cup of juice)

Breads

Banana and Walnut Bread

This delicious no rise bread is a favorite in our family. Make sure the bananas are slightly under-ripe so you don't add too much sugar content.

1 cup whole grain flour
½ cup oat flour
½ cup walnuts, divided
1 tsp baking powder
1 tsp baking soda
1 tsp cinnamon
½ tsp nutmeg
½ tsp xanthan gum
¼ tsp salt
3 bananas (slightly green at ends), mashed
½ cup agave nectar
1/3 cup plain soymilk
¼ cup canola oil
2 tsp pure vanilla extract

Procedure

Prepare an 8 x 4 inch bread pan by coating with grease.

Combine flours, walnuts (conserve 2Tbs for topping), baking powder, baking soda, cinnamon, nutmeg, xanthan gum and salt in a large bowl.

Place bananas, agave nectar, soymilk, oil and vanilla in a blender are process until just smooth.

Pour the banana mixture into the flour mixture and fold in.

Pour batter into the greased pan. Top with reserved walnuts.

Yield: 1 loaf

Nutrition Facts

Serving size: 1 slice (about 1/12th of a loaf)

Amount Per Serving	
Calories	202.77
Calories From Fat (35%)	71.07
	% Daily Value
Total Fat 8.23g	**13%**
Saturated Fat 0.75g	**4%**
Cholesterol 0mg	**0%**
Sodium 199.22mg	**8%**
Potassium 184.78mg	**5%**
Total Carbohydrates 31.36g	**10%**
Fiber 2.08g	**8%**
Sugar 15.88g	
Protein 3.05g	**6%**

Flour Tortillas

This authentic Mexican recipe was given to me by a Mexican doctor who recommended it as a healthy alternative to white tortillas.

1	tsp	baking powder
1	cup	hot water
½	cup	vegetable lard
4	cups	whole wheat flour
1	tsp	salt

Procedure

Put the flour in the bowl, adding the salt, baking powder, and lard, mix it with your fingers until it is crumbly.

Add the hot water -not boiling- , mix with your hands until you have a homogeneous, very sticky, dough. Add up to 1 cup more water if necessary (this will depend on the type of flour you use).

Cover with a clean cloth and let it rest for about 2 hrs.

Gently knead until smooth and separate into 24 equal pieces, knead the pieces with your hands until they are smooth again and cover again.

Heat the grill, extend one by one the pieces over a board with the baking pin to make round discs, lift carefully with your fingers and place on the heated grill.

Lower the flame to medium heat, leave for about 2 minutes -lift one end if it has a golden color you may turn it around to cook on the other side.

Once you do this, you may see that the tortilla inflates, depending on your own preferences.

You may leave it until it deflates by itself or push it down.

You may add some more fiber by reducing the amount of flour, 1 ½ cups whole wheat flour and ½ cup of bran wheat, just remember that the altitude in your city will require adjustment of the baking powder.

To add more or less liquid - the batter should be firm, but moist, and with the standing time and the fat it should be elastic but not sticky; as with all batters, add a little more flour if needed.

Yield: 24 medium tortillas

Nutrition Facts

Serving size: 1 tortilla.

Amount Per Serving	
Calories	38.92
Calories From Fat (99%)	38.45
	% Daily Value
Total Fat 4.27g	7%
Saturated Fat 1.72g	9%
Cholesterol 2.39mg	<1%
Sodium 117.21mg	5%
Potassium 0.17mg	<1%
Total Carbohydrates 0.13g	<1%
Fiber 0g	0%
Sugar 0g	
Protein 0.01g	<1%

Simple Whole Wheat Bread

I use a bread machine with this recipe. Just throw the ingredients in and go! I recommend you get one, otherwise avoiding supermarket breads will be a chore.

3	cups	warm water
2	pkg.	active dry yeast
1/3	cup	honey
3	cups	bread flour
5	tbsp	butter, melted
1/3	cup	honey
1	tbsp	salt
5 ½	cups	whole wheat flour

Procedure

Place ingredients in a bread machine according to manufacturers instructions.

Bake on whole wheat cycle.

Yield: 3 loaves

Nutrition Facts

Serving size: 1/10 of a loaf

Amount Per Serving	
Calories	175.1
Calories From Fat (12%)	20.98
	% Daily Value
Total Fat 2.41g	**4%**
Saturated Fat 1.29g	**6%**
Cholesterol 5.09mg	**2%**
Sodium 234.95mg	**10%**
Potassium 58.99mg	**2%**
Total Carbohydrates 33.94g	**11%**
Fiber 1.13g	**5%**
Sugar 6.29g	
Protein 4.36g	**9%**

Whole Wheat Pizza Base

I cook all my pizzas using a pizza stone. You can purchase one for under $20; it's the difference between your pizza tasting home-made and authentic--pizzas off a baking sheet just don't cook the same way.

1 tsp fructose

1 ½ cups warm water

1 packet dried yeast

1 Tbsp olive oil

1 tsp salt

2 cups whole wheat flour

1 ½ cups all purpose flour

Procedure

Place all ingredients in a bread machine on the dough cycle.

Roll out to 12" circle.

See Thai Chikin Pizza for cooking instructions.

Yield: 1 pizza base

Nutrition Facts

Serving size: 1/16th of a pizza

Amount Per Serving	
Calories	145.73
Calories From Fat (9%)	13.17
	% Daily Value
Total Fat 1.51g	**2%**
Saturated Fat 0.22g	**1%**
Cholesterol 0mg	**0%**
Sodium 195.72mg	**8%**
Potassium 51.03mg	**1%**
Total Carbohydrates 28.39g	**9%**
Fiber 1.11g	**4%**
Sugar 0.45g	
Protein 3.99g	**8%**

Whole Wheat Puff Pastry

The possibilities for fillings are endless: just make sure you use protein in the filling, as the pastry has a fair serving of carbs.

3/4	cup	whole wheat flour
3/4	cup	all purpose flour
3/4	tbs	sugar
3/4	tsp	salt
6 oz		butter
1	tsp	lemon juice
4 ½	tbs	very cold water

Procedure

Place flour, sugar and salt into a medium sized bowl. Cut the (chilled) butter into ¼" square cubes and add to flour.

Combine water and lemon juice in a small bowl. Add ½ of the mixture to the flour/butter mixture and toss with a spatula until the juice soaks in. Add remaining liquid one tablespoon at a time.

Roll pastry quickly into a 15" strip. Fold ends to the center. Fold in half again.

Turn pastry 90 degrees. Roll the air out with a rolling pin.

Repeat step 2 and 3 four times.

Best used immediately.

Yield: Enough pastry for 1 pie

Nutrition Facts

Serving size: 1/10 recipe

Amount Per Serving	
Calories	51.6
Calories From Fat (2%)	1.16
	% Daily Value
Total Fat 0.14g	**<1%**
Saturated Fat 0.02g	**<1%**
Cholesterol 0mg	**0%**
Sodium 218.3mg	**9%**
Potassium 15.21mg	**<1%**
Total Carbohydrates 10.82g	**4%**
Fiber 0.38g	**2%**
Sugar 0.04g	
Protein 1.46g	3%

Breakfasts

Fruit Smoothies

Smoothies for breakfast are a staple in our house. The cashews and spinach add needed protein to make sure you don't have too many carbs.

2 Tbs Flax seeds (soaked 3 hours)

1 cup cashews (soaked 3 hours)

4 cups water

1 Banana, frozen and sliced into 1" pieces

1 cup Frozen berry mix

2 cups spinach,uncooked

¼ cup dates (soaked 3 hours)

Procedure

Place flax seeds, cashews, and water in blender.

Blend until well creamy.

Add fruit, spinach, and dates.

Blend until smooth.

Yield: 2 smoothies

Nutrition Facts

Serving size: 1 smoothie

Amount Per Serving	
Calories	387.12
Calories From Fat (26%)	99.59
	% Daily Value
Total Fat 11.9g	**18%**
Saturated Fat 1.67g	**8%**
Cholesterol 0mg	**0%**
Sodium 48.01mg	**2%**
Potassium 884.19mg	**25%**
Total Carbohydrates 69.29g	**23%**
Fiber 10.09g	**40%**
Sugar 22.46g	
Protein 8.6g	**17%**

French Toast with Flax Seed and Blackberries

½ cup raw cashew pieces
1 ½ Tbsp cornstarch
2 Tbsp whole flaxseed
1 ½ tsp vanilla extract
¼ tsp salt
⅛ tsp ground cinnamon or coriander
6 slices Ezekiel 4:9 Sprouted Grain bread or sourdough bread
1 cup blackberries
1 tsp agave syrup

Procedure

Blend all ingredients except for toast until creamy, about 3-4 minutes.

Dip slices of bread into mixture and fry as you would regular French toast, until crispy (3-4 minutes).

Blend ¼ cup of the berries with the agave syrup. Add remainder of berries and stir. Microwave for 30-45 seconds. Use in place of syrup.

Yield: 6 slices

Nutrition Facts

Serving size: 1/3 of a recipe
(2.8 ounces).

Amount Per Serving	
Calories	294.87
Calories From Fat (41%)	121.54
	% Daily Value
Total Fat 13.81g	**21%**
Saturated Fat 1.77g	**9%**
Cholesterol 0mg	**0%**
Sodium 459.98mg	**19%**
Potassium 179.92mg	**5%**
Total Carbohydrates 32.75g	**11%**
Fiber 4.95g	**20%**
Sugar 4.57g	
Protein 9.3g	**19%**

Golden Whole Wheat Crepes

These thin pancakes can be filled with any fruit. Serve these pancakes with scrambled eggs to get the protein with this meal.

3/4 cup whole wheat flour

¼ tsp salt

½ tsp baking powder

enough soy milk to make a smooth batter

1 kiwifruit, sliced

1 orange

4 Tbsp orange juice

¼ cup honey

Procedure

Sift flour, salt and baking powder into a large bowl.

Add milk, whisking until a smooth batter forms.

Cook on a hot griddle until bubbling and edges are light brown.

Peel orange and remove slices. Skin, removing seeds and membranes.

Lightly boil orange juice and honey in a small saucepan for 4 minutes.

To serve, put one tablespoon of fruit in one pancake, fold over and drizzle honey syrup on top.

Servings: 2

Nutrition Facts

Serving size: 4 pancakes

Amount Per Serving	
Calories	457.45
Calories From Fat (6%)	27.21
	% Daily Value
Total Fat 3.09g	**5%**
Saturated Fat 0.36g	**2%**
Cholesterol 0mg	**0%**
Sodium 481.36mg	**20%**
Potassium 584.73mg	**17%**
Total Carbohydrates 100.95g	**34%**
Fiber 7.27g	**29%**
Sugar 42.38g	
Protein 10.64g	**21%**

Granola Bars

The trouble with store-purchased granola bars for reactive hypoglycemics is that they tend to be carb-heavy and laden with sugar. These bars are balanced. Make them on Sunday and they will last for a week in the fridge.

1-2 apples

1 ½ cups pitted dates (soaked for 3 hours)

½ cup agave nectar

2 Tbsp lemon juice, fresh

2 Tbsp orange extract or zest

1 Tbsp vanilla extract

1 tsp ground cinnamon

2 tsp sea salt

7 cups mixed raw nuts (coarsely chopped) and seeds soaked overnight and rinsed well (walnuts, almonds, sunflower seeds, etc)

1 cup dried cranberries (apple juice sweetened)

Procedure

In food processor, place apples, dates, agave, lemon juice, orange extract, vanilla, cinnamon, salt, and process until completely smooth. Transfer to a large bowl.

Add nuts and seeds. Mix well.

Spread on a baking sheet and bake at 350 degrees until crunchy (about 20-25 minutes).

Yield: 10 cups or 40 bars

Nutrition Facts

Serving size: 1 bar

Amount Per Serving	
Calories	231.14
Calories From Fat (46%)	106.37
	% Daily Value
Total Fat 12.67g	**19%**
Saturated Fat 1.66g	**8%**
Cholesterol 0mg	**0%**
Sodium 1097.4mg	**46%**
Potassium 201.4mg	**6%**
Total Carbohydrates 27.86g	**9%**
Fiber 3.86g	**15%**
Sugar 8.13g	
Protein 4.41g	**9%**

Great Breakfast Burritos

Use the whole wheat tortilla recipe from this book for this breakfast staple. They can be frozen and microwaved for 2 mins to reheat.

12-16 oz extra firm tofu, drained, pressed and crumbled OR 12 oz lean ground beef

1 ea small yellow onion, peeled and diced

2 ea garlic cloves, minced or pressed

1 ea bell pepper, diced

2 ea small red potatoes

4 Tbsp olive oil

½ tsp turmeric

1 pinch salt

1 pinch pepper

6 tortillas

½ cup mushrooms, quartered or sliced (optional)

1 ea jalapeno, sliced

1 cup red, yellow peppers, diced

2 ea breakfast sausage patties, diced

½ cup cheese, grated

6 Tbsp fresh salsa

Procedure

Preheat oven to 375° Fahrenheit.

Chop the potatoes into bite sized pieces. Place in a Ziplock bag with 1T olive oil and a dash of salt and pepper.

Bake potatoes for 20 minutes.

While waiting for potatoes to cook, heat 3T olive oil in a frying pan.

Add garlic and vegetables. Cook on medium heat until the onions are softened.

Add tofu and turmeric.

Add sausage. Cook for 5 minutes, stirring occasionally until sausage is heated through.

Place warm tortilla on a plate. Fill with 1/6 of the tofu mixture and 1T of salsa.

Divide the cheese between the burritos. Roll up and enjoy!

Yield: 6 Burritos

Nutrition Facts

Serving size: 1 burrito

Amount Per Serving	
Calories	355.93
Calories From Fat (44%)	156.63
	% Daily Value
Total Fat 17.71g	**27%**
Saturated Fat 2.65g	**13%**
Cholesterol 7.33mg	**2%**
Sodium 536.91mg	**22%**
Potassium 448.2mg	**13%**
Total Carbohydrates 38.58g	**13%**
Fiber 2.18g	**9%**
Sugar 2.2g	
Protein 12.07g	**24%**

Tangy Breakfast Scramble

This scramble will fill you up so much you probably won't feel like that mid morning snack! Nutritional yeast contains B-12 and can be found in health food stores.

For the sauce:

½ cup flour
½ cup nutritional yeast
1 tsp garlic powder
2 cups water
1 tsp yellow mustard
4 tbsp or less margarine

For the stir fry:

½ onion
4 strips bacon OR veggie bacon
½ green pepper
6 ea eggs, free range
3 Tbs olive oil
Salt and pepper, to taste

Procedure

Mix flour, nutritional yeast, garlic powder, and water in a small saucepan. Heat on medium until thick and bubbling.

Remove from heat. Add mustard and margarine.

Sauté onion and green pepper in 1T olive oil for 3-4 minutes until soft.

Add 2T more oil.

Add whisked eggs.

While eggs are cooking, microwave bacon until crispy (add 30 seconds to the suggested package timing).

Sauté this for another couple of minutes.

Add salt and pepper to taste.

Add crumbled bacon, salt and pepper, and sauce from small saucepan. Sauté for 2 minutes and serve.

Yield: 4 servings

Nutrition Facts

Serving size: 1 cup

Amount Per Serving	
Calories	159.28
Calories From Fat (58%)	91.64
	% Daily Value
Total Fat 10.38g	**16%**
Saturated Fat 1.44g	**7%**
Cholesterol 0mg	**0%**
Sodium 19.59mg	**<1%**
Potassium 81.49mg	**2%**
Total Carbohydrates 14.77g	**5%**
Fiber 1.1g	**4%**
Sugar 1.31g	
Protein 2.11g	**4%**

Whole Wheat Pumpkin Muffins

These are so delicious, you'll feel like you can eat more than one. You can find fructose in any health food store. It's a great substitute for sugar in baking.

1 15oz canned pumpkin
3/4 cup olive oil
1 cup whole wheat flour
½ cup oat bran
½ cup quick oats
1 scoop soy protein powder
2 ½ tsp teaspoon baking powder
1 ½ tsp baking soda
½ tsp salt
1 ½ tsp cinnamon
½ tsp nutmeg
½ tsp cloves
1 tsp vanilla
¼ cup vanilla soy milk
3/4 cup fructose

Procedure

Place pumpkin, oil, and fructose in a large bowl and mix well.

Combine flour, oat bran, oats, protein powder, baking powder, baking soda, salt, cinnamon, nutmeg and cloves in a large bowl.

Add ½ cup of the dry mixture at a time to the pumpkin mix, stirring well between each addition.

Add vanilla and soy milk.

Fill the muffin cups to 3/4 full.

Bake for 20-25 minutes.

Yield: 12 small muffins

Nutrition Facts

Serving size: 1 muffin

Amount Per Serving	
Calories	224.33
Calories From Fat (55%)	123.99
	% Daily Value
Total Fat 14.05g	**22%**
Saturated Fat 1.09g	**5%**
Cholesterol 0mg	**0%**
Sodium 359.69mg	**15%**
Potassium 32.95mg	**<1%**
Total Carbohydrates 23.6g	**8%**
Fiber 0.88g	**4%**
Sugar 12.65g	
Protein 1.68g	**3%**

Desserts

Strawberry Shortcake

One of the hardest things about being on a sugar-restricted diet is that you often miss out on old favorites, like sweets. This strawberry shortcake will aid in satiating that sweet tooth! This recipe will yield a half dozen extra biscuits which can be frozen for up to a month.

½ cup whole wheat flour

½ cup whole wheat pastry flour

1 ½ Tbsp nutritional Yeast Flakes

2 Tbsp baking powder

½ tsp sea salt

¼ tsp garlic powder

3 Tbsp vegan buttery spread, cut into 4-5 pieces

½ cup soy milk

½ tsp vinegar

2 cups fresh strawberries

⅓ cup frozen strawberries

2 Tbsp floral honey

8 Tbsp whipped, canned cream (no sugar added)

Procedure

Place flours, yeast flakes, baking powder, sea salt, garlic powder and buttery spread in a food processor and process to chunky crumbs (if you do not have a food processor, rub in the butter by hand).

Add milk to crumb mixture, stir until moistened.

Drop large tablespoons of the mix onto a greased baking sheet. Bake for 10-12 minutes until light brown.

Place frozen strawberries and honey in a blender. Blend for 1 minute. Mix with quartered fresh strawberries.

Cut open biscuit. Place ¼ of the strawberry mix on biscuit, top with whipped cream.

Yield: 4 shortcakes

Nutrition Facts

Serving size: ¼ of a recipe (5.8 ounces).

Amount Per Serving	
Calories	159.67
Calories From Fat (34%)	54.38
	% Daily Value
Total Fat 6.09g	**9%**
Saturated Fat 1.99g	**10%**
Cholesterol 4.56mg	**2%**
Sodium 1052.23mg	**44%**
Potassium 212.33mg	**6%**
Total Carbohydrates 24.46g	**8%**
Fiber 2.54g	**10%**
Sugar 6.43g	
Protein 3.42g	**7%**

Blackberry and Peach Sorbet

3		bananas
5	cups	mixed blackberries and peaches

Procedure

Thaw frozen fruit for 30 minutes. While fruit is thawing, freeze bananas for 30 minutes.

Pulse in a food processor for 1 minute, ensuring chunks are processed.

Serve immediately, or freeze for 1 hour for a harder consistency.

Yield: 12 servings

Nutrition Facts

Serving size: 1/12 of a recipe (5.1 ounces).

Amount Per Serving	
Calories	100.89
Calories From Fat (5%)	4.78
	% Daily Value
Total Fat 0.57g	**<1%**
Saturated Fat 0.1g	**<1%**
Cholesterol 0mg	**0%**
Sodium 1.44mg	**<1%**
Potassium 399.26mg	**11%**
Total Carbohydrates 25.04g	**8%**
Fiber 5.37g	**21%**
Sugar 13.25g	
Protein 1.75g	**4%**

Apple, Cranberry, and Pear Crisp

This treat is best eaten in small portions after a protein heavy dinner.

2		red apples - peeled, cored, and cubed
2		pears - peeled, cored, and cubed
½	cup	dried cranberries
1	tbsp	all-purpose flour
2	tbsp	honey
1 ½	tbsp	lemon juice
½	cup	whole wheat flour
½	cup	fructose
½	cup	quick cooking oats
¼	cup	ground walnuts
½	cup	butter

Procedure

Grease an 8" round baking dish with butter.

Mix the apples, pears, cranberries, 1 tablespoon flour, honey, and lemon juice in the baking dish.

Combine the remaining ingredients in a small bowl and sprinkle over the fruit mixture.

Bake until golden brown.

Nutrition Facts

Servings: 16

Amount Per Serving	
Calories	210.42
Calories From Fat (31%)	65.43
	% Daily Value
Total Fat 7.51g	**12%**
Saturated Fat 3.8g	**19%**
Cholesterol 15.25mg	**5%**
Sodium 4.22mg	**<1%**
Potassium 94.06mg	3%
Total Carbohydrates 35.98g	**12%**
Fiber 2.94g	**12%**
Sugar 13.3g	
Protein 1.29g	3%

Avocado Chocolate Dream Pie

You won't believe that the base for this pie is avocado. Forget those supermarket, sugar-laden pies: this one's a dream!

2		large avocados
2	cups	vegan chocolate chips (try Tropical Source chips)
1/8	cup	soy milk
1	tbsp	vanilla extract
2	tbsp	agave syrup
		Arrowhead mills pie crust
½	cup	frozen raspberries
1	tbsp	orange juice

Procedure

Sprinkle raspberries onto pie crust.

Melt chocolate chips in a microwave. Add soy milk, vanilla, and agave syrup. Mix well and cool in fridge.

While chocolate is cooling, peel and mash avocado until smooth.

Add orange juice to avocado and stir well.

Add chocolate mix to avocados. Stir well.

Pour over raspberries and place in fridge to set.

Top with whipped cream.

Yield: 1 pie

Nutrition Facts

Servings: 4

Amount Per Serving	
Calories	305.51
Calories From Fat (48%)	148.08
	% Daily Value
Total Fat 17.79g	**27%**
Saturated Fat 6.61g	**33%**
Cholesterol 0mg	**0%**
Sodium 119.03mg	**5%**
Potassium 184.25mg	**5%**
Total Carbohydrates 39.06g	**13%**
Fiber 4.4g	**18%**
Sugar 13.09g	
Protein 2.74g	**5%**

Chocolate Chip Cookies

Check the ingredients in the chocolate chips you use for this recipe: you don't want sugary chocolate chips that you find in the regular grocery store. Try finding carob chocolate chips in a health food store or dark chocolate chips, which contain less sugar. Grind the oats beforehand in a food processor.

1	Tbs	butter
3/4	cup	rolled oats, ground
1	cup	whole-wheat flour
½	tsp	baking soda
½	tsp	salt
¼	cup	butter, softened
¼	cup	canola oil
½	cup	fructose
1		large egg
1	tsp	vanilla extract
1	cup	chocolate chips

Procedure

Prepare a baking sheet by coating with a thin layer of butter.

Place oats, flour, baking soda, and salt in a large bowl. Mix well.

Beat butter and egg until creamed.

Add oil, fructose and vanilla. Continue beating until well combined.

Stir in flour mix slowly.

Stir in chocolate chips.

Drop dough in 1Tbsp rounds onto a cookie sheet.

Bake until golden brown.

Yield: makes about 2 ½ dozen cookies

Nutrition Facts

Serving size: 1 cookie

Amount Per Serving	
Calories	96.76
Calories From Fat (51%)	49.55
	% Daily Value
Total Fat 5.79g	**9%**
Saturated Fat 2.43g	**12%**
Cholesterol 12.13mg	**4%**
Sodium 63.28mg	**3%**
Potassium 26.61mg	**<1%**
Total Carbohydrates 11.19g	**4%**
Fiber 1.02g	**4%**
Sugar 3.4g	
Protein 1.28g	3%

Chocolate Crispy Bars

Why use vegan chocolate chips? They tend to be sweetened with fructose or evaporated cane sugar, which is easier on the blood sugar. But you can use any type of chocolate chips without sugar or high fructose corn syrup.

½ cup almond butter

¾ cup honey

½ cup chopped almonds

½ cup vegan chocolate chips

3 cups crispy brown rice cereal (check ingredients for no sugar or high fructose)

Procedure

Prepare a 9" square pan by coating lightly with butter.

In a large saucepan, melt almond butter, agave syrup, and chocolate chips together.

Remove from heat.

Stir in crisped rice and chopped almonds.

Press into pan and allow to cool before cutting into squares.

Yield: 16 pieces

Nutrition Facts

Serving size: 1 piece

Amount Per Serving	
Calories	171.93
Calories From Fat (42%)	72.06
	% Daily Value
Total Fat 8.68g	**13%**
Saturated Fat 1.59g	**8%**
Cholesterol 0mg	**0%**
Sodium 37.13mg	**2%**
Potassium 113.93mg	**3%**
Total Carbohydrates 24.07g	**8%**
Fiber 1.58g	**6%**
Sugar 14.19g	
Protein 2.82g	**6%**

Mocha Ice Cream with Saffron Cream Sauce

This recipe came from a raw food meet we recently went to. If you aren't familiar with raw food, the concept is that raw food retains more nutrients and actually makes you feel better. I'm personally not sure yet if the raw food lifestyle is for me, but I do know this ice cream tastes fabulous--and it's good for you! Our ice cream maker is a hand-churn style and we purchased it for less than $15 on eBay.

Chocolate Ice Cream

2	cups	coconut meat
2	cups	coconut water
1	cup	almond milk
1	cup	peeled Truly Raw cacao beans (powdered)
1/3	cup	mesquite pod meal
2	tbsp	Carob Powder
¾	cup	agave nectar
3	tbsp	Coconut Oil
1	tsp	sea salt or to taste

Saffron Cream Sauce

1	cup	young coconut meat
¾	cup	almond milk
1/3	cup	agave nectar
		pinch of salt
2	tsp	saffron

Procedure

Soak the saffron in 3 tbs. of soy milk. Let sit while preparing ice cream.

Blend all the ice cream ingredients together in a food processor. Strain through a wire mesh sieve.

Transfer to an ice cream maker and follow manufacturer's instructions.

Add the remaining ingredients into the food processor and process until smooth.

Yield: 12 servings

Nutrition Facts

Serving size: ½ cup

Amount Per Serving	
Calories	302.26
Calories From Fat (48%)	143.7
	% Daily Value
Total Fat 17.02g	**26%**
Saturated Fat 9.97g	**50%**
Cholesterol 0mg	**0%**
Sodium 1940.22mg	**81%**
Potassium 367.22mg	**10%**
Total Carbohydrates 40.92g	**14%**
Fiber 5.67g	**23%**
Sugar 30.13g	
Protein 4.24g	**8%**

Raw Ice Cream

1	cup	raw cashews
1		banana
1	cup	frozen fruit

Procedure

Place all ingredients into a food processor and blend.

Serve immediately.

Yield: 4 servings

Nutrition Facts

Serving size: 1cup

Amount Per Serving	
Calories	173.99
Calories From Fat (47%)	82.12
	% Daily Value
Total Fat 9.82g	**15%**
Saturated Fat 0.97g	**5%**
Cholesterol 0mg	**0%**
Sodium 0.88mg	**<1%**
Potassium 358.74mg	**10%**
Total Carbohydrates 22.04g	**7%**
Fiber 3.5g	**14%**
Sugar 11.83g	
Protein 3.34g	**7%**

The Best Chocolate Chip Cookies in the World

3	tbsp	olive oil
2	cups	walnuts, ground
2/3	cup	fructose
2	tsp	vanilla extract
1 ½	cups	oat flour
1	tsp	baking soda
1	tsp	salt
¼	tsp	ground cinnamon
2	cups	rolled oats
12 oz		vegan chocolate chips

Procedure

Place olive oil and walnuts into a mixing bowl. Whisk (best done with an electric mixer) until blended.

Place ½ cup water in a saucepan. Bring to a boil.

Add mixture to mixing bowl. Mix well.

Add vanilla, oat flour, baking soda, salt, and cinnamon to mix and continue mixing.

Fold in remaining ingredients.

Chill for 20 minutes. Roll out into a log shape (1″ thick). Slice into 1″ thick pieces.

Bake 10 minutes in a 350°F oven.

Yield: makes 30 cookies

Nutrition Facts

Serving size: 1 cookie

Amount Per Serving	
Calories	132.68
Calories From Fat (45%)	59.43
	% Daily Value
Total Fat 7.02g	**11%**
Saturated Fat 0.68g	**3%**
Cholesterol 0mg	**0%**
Sodium 122.69mg	**5%**
Potassium 98.84mg	**3%**
Total Carbohydrates 16.21g	**5%**
Fiber 1.68g	**7%**
Sugar 7.56g	
Protein 2.67g	**5%**

Healthy Cookie Recipe

Make sure you stick to the serving size (1) of these cookies. They are healthful, but sweet!

3		bananas, mashed (select bananas slightly green at one end)
1	tsp	vanilla extract
¼	cup	olive oil
2	cups	rolled oats
2/3	cup	almond meal
1/3	cup	coconut, finely shredded & unsweetened
½	tsp	cinnamon
½	tsp	fine grain sea salt
1	tsp	baking powder
¾	cup	vegan chocolate chips

Procedure

Combine bananas, vanilla extract, and coconut oil in a large bowl.

In a separate bowl, mix oats, almond meal, shredded coconut, cinnamon, salt, and baking powder together.

Combine the two bowls and stir well.

Add chocolate chips and stir.

Drop 1Tbs of the mixture onto a greased and floured baking sheet.

Bake until golden brown.

Yield: 3 dozen bite-sized cookies

Nutrition Facts

Serving size: 1 cookie

Amount Per Serving	
Calories	63.98
Calories From Fat (42%)	26.92
	% Daily Value
Total Fat 3.18g	5%
Saturated Fat 1.11g	6%
Cholesterol 0mg	0%
Sodium 53.52mg	2%
Potassium 58.04mg	2%
Total Carbohydrates 8.79g	3%
Fiber 1.09g	4%
Sugar 1.85g	
Protein 0.96g	2%

Tofu Pumpkin Pie

You won't have to go without pie this Thanksgiving with this hypoglycemic-friendly pie. You won't notice the difference--honest! The tofu adds protein, making it okay to have a slightly larger portion.

16	oz	pureed pumpkin
½	cup	fructose
½	tsp	salt
1	tsp	ground cinnamon
½	tsp	ground ginger
¼	tsp	ground cloves
1	tsp	ground allspice, optional
½	tsp	ground nutmeg, optional
2-3	tbsp	cornstarch
1	10-12 oz pkg.	silken/soft tofu
1	9-in	unbaked whole wheat pie shell
1	pint	whipping cream

Procedure

Pulse the pumpkin and fructose in a food processor for 15 seconds.

Add remaining pie ingredients and pulse until mixed well.

Pour pie filling into shell. Bake for 15 minutes.

Reduce heat to 350° and cook for 60 more minutes.

Best served cold with whipped cream.

Yield: 1 pie

Nutrition Facts

Serving size: 1/6th of a pie.

Amount Per Serving	
Calories	296.8
Calories From Fat (69%)	203.56
	% Daily Value
Total Fat 23.13g	**36%**
Saturated Fat 14.08g	**70%**
Cholesterol 81.52mg	**27%**
Sodium 335.62mg	**14%**
Potassium 195.08mg	**6%**
Total Carbohydrates 21.79g	**7%**
Fiber 2.09g	**8%**
Sugar 14.81g	
Protein 2.8g	**6%**

Vegan Cheesecake

I am lactose intolerant so cannot eat regular cream cheese. You'll notice no difference between a vegan version of the cheesecake and its sugary counterpart. Find Ener-G egg replacer in your local health food store.

1 ea Arrowhead Mills pre-made pie crust

16 ounces Tofutti Better Than Cream Cheese

1/3 cup Fructose

4 EnerG egg substitute "eggs"

1 tsp vanilla

juice of one lemon

1 can whipped cream

fresh raspberries

Procedure

Combine cream cheese, fructose, eggs, vanilla, and lemon juice in a blender. Blend until smooth.

Pour into crust. Bake until set.

Cool, then place in refrigerator overnight.

Serve with whipped cream and a raspberry on top. Yield: 1 pie

Nutrition Facts

Serving size: 1/12th pie

Amount Per Serving	
Calories	133.65
Calories From Fat (55%)	73.58
	% Daily Value
Total Fat 8.15g	**13%**
Saturated Fat 4.95g	**25%**
Cholesterol 25.06mg	**8%**
Sodium 139.39mg	**6%**
Potassium 111.47mg	**3%**
Total Carbohydrates 9.88g	**3%**
Fiber 0.14g	**<1%**
Sugar 5.99g	
Protein 5.38g	**11%**

Dinners

Portabella Mushroom Burgers

2 ea garlic clove, chopped
6 Tbsp olive oil
½ tsp thyme
2 Tbsp balsamic vinegar
1 pinch salt
1 pinch black pepper
4 ea Portobello mushroom caps
4 ea whole grain or sprouted grain burger buns
1 Tbsp capers, finely chopped
¼ cup Vegenaise spread or Mayonnaise spread
1 ea tomato
4 ea romaine lettuce leaves

Procedure

Preheat broiler.

Whisk together garlic, olive oil, thyme, vinegar, salt, and pepper.

Rinse mushroom caps. Place mushrooms under broiler in a broiler pan.

Baste mushrooms with ½ the liquid. Broil for 5 minutes.

Turn mushrooms over, baste with remaining liquid. Broil for 5 minutes. Place buns under broiler in last 2 minutes and broil 1 min each side.

Mix mayonnaise and capers. Assemble burger, bun, dressing and fixings.

Yield: 4 burgers

Nutrition Facts

Serving size: 1 burger

Amount Per Serving	
Calories	282.06
Calories From Fat (43%)	121.28
	% Daily Value
Total Fat 13.66g	**21%**
Saturated Fat 1.98g	**10%**
Cholesterol 5.04mg	**2%**
Sodium 539.99mg	**22%**
Potassium 292.42mg	**8%**
Total Carbohydrates 31.36g	**10%**
Fiber 5.73g	**23%**
Sugar 5.36g	
Protein 9.18g	**18%**

Nacho Salad

For guacamole:

1		small avocado
1 ½	cups	silken tofu, soft
¼	tsp	salt
1	pinch	black pepper
1	pinch	cayenne pepper
¼	tsp	garlic clove, minced
⅛	tsp	cumin
2	Tbsp	lemon juice

For nachos:

3	cups	baked, whole-grain tortilla chips
4	cups	iceburg lettuce, shredded
1	can	black beans, drained
1	cup	Mexican blend shredded cheese
1 ½	cups	salsa
4	ea	scallions, chopped

Procedure

Blend guacamole ingredients for 3-4 minutes until creamy.

In a serving bowl, layer the chips, lettuce, beans, cheese, salsa, and scallions. Top with the guacamole and serve.

Yield: 8 cups

Nutrition Facts

Amount Per Serving	
Calories	527.41
Calories From Fat (36%)	192.49
	% Daily Value
Total Fat 22.13g	**34%**
Saturated Fat 5.68g	**28%**
Cholesterol 16.92mg	**6%**
Sodium 1539.02mg	**64%**
Potassium 1352.52mg	**39%**
Total Carbohydrates 67.35g	**22%**
Fiber 15.81g	**63%**
Sugar 6.98g	
Protein 21.16g	**42%**

Serving size: ¼ recipe

Southern Fried Popcorn Chik'n

Pinch ea. Salt and pepper
½ tsp onion powder
1 tsp paprika
1 tsp garlic powder
1 cup unbleached white flour
1 cup whole wheat flour
3 Tbsp yellow mustard
2 Tbsp. baking powder
1 bag Quorn Chik'n chunks or chicken, cut into 1" chunks OR 1lb chicken, cut into chunks
4 cups olive oil

Procedure

Mix salt, onion powder, pepper, paprika, garlic powder, and flour in a large bowl.

Defrost Quorn in microwave for about 10 minutes.

Mix mustard and water together in a large bowl. Add ½ of flour mixture to bowl and stir well. Place Chik'n chunks in mustard bowl and mix well until coated.

Place ¼ of the Quorn into the flour & toss, ensuring all sides covered.

Deep fry in olive oil until crispy and brown, about 3-4 minutes. Repeat for remaining product.

Nutrition Facts

Serving size: 1/6 recipe (3.7 ounces).

Amount Per Serving	
Calories	253.48
Calories From Fat (27%)	68.16
	% Daily Value
Total Fat 7.73g	**12%**
Saturated Fat 1.06g	**5%**
Cholesterol 0.47mg	**<1%**
Sodium 701.41mg	**29%**
Potassium 118.47mg	**3%**
Total Carbohydrates 37.3g	**12%**
Fiber 2.61g	**10%**
Sugar 0.56g	
Protein 8.94g	**18%**

Tomato Quiche

This bakes more like a thick crust pie than a quiche. However, even my finicky ten-year-old gave this dish the thumbs up! If you prefer, substitute mushrooms or onions in place of the tomatoes. For meat eaters, a slice or two of chopped bacon sprinkled on top will add flavor.

1	cup	whole wheat bread crumbs
¼	cup	whole wheat flour
½	cup	bulgur or cracked wheat
½	cup	Toasted Oats
¼	tsp	salt
¾	tsp	marjoram
½	cup	vegan buttery spread, melted
1	Tbsp	olive oil
1	ea	sliced tomato (large)
½	tsp	thyme
¼	lb	sharp cheddar, grated
2	ea	eggs
⅛	cup	egg whites (try Organic Valley)
1	cup	soy milk
½	tsp	paprika

Procedure

Preheat oven to 350 degrees. Mix whole wheat bread crumbs, whole wheat flour, bulgur wheat, salt, toasted oats, and ¼ tsp of the marjoram, together in a large bowl. Add buttery spread and mix well.

Press into a 8" pie dish. Bake for 10 minutes.

Sprinkle grated cheddar over crust.

Saute mushrooms, scallions, thyme, and oregano in olive oil for 3 minutes until softened. Pour evenly into pie.

Whisk eggs, egg white, and milk. Pour over mushrooms.

Top with sprinkled paprika.

Bake at 375 degrees for 40 minutes until golden brown.

Yield: 1 quiche

Nutrition Facts

Serving size: 1/8 of a recipe (3.9 ounces).

Amount Per Serving	
Calories	215.19
Calories From Fat (44%)	95.1
	% Daily Value
Total Fat 10.66g	**16%**
Saturated Fat 2.75g	**14%**
Cholesterol 54.81mg	**18%**
Sodium 317.14mg	**13%**
Potassium 171.14mg	**5%**
Total Carbohydrates 22.03g	**7%**
Fiber 2.12g	**8%**
Sugar 2.36g	
Protein 7.91g	**16%**

Andrew's Veggie Lasagna

My fourteen-year-old son made this dish for a Friday night supper with friends. It was such a hit, even my friends wanted the recipe!

6 ea whole wheat lasagna noodles

2 Tbsp olive oil

½ cup onion, finely chopped

1 ea garlic clove, minced

1 tsp oregano, fresh

2 tsp basil, fresh

½ tsp black pepper

1 cup zucchini, diced

1 cup mushrooms, diced

3 cups spinach

For Ricotta Filling:

6 ea Roma tomato, chopped

1 lb firm tofu

⅛ cup lemon juice

2 tsp xylitol

½ tsp salt

2 tsp basil

2 Tbsp olive oil

½ tsp garlic clove, minced

Procedure

Cook noodles according to package directions.

Stir fry onion and garlic in olive oil for 4 minutes until softened.

Puree tomatoes in a blender. Add to onion and garlic. Add oregano, basil, pepper, zucchini, mushrooms, and spinach. Simmer for 10 minutes.

Place Ricotta filling ingredients in a large bowl and mash well.

Spray a 13" x 9" lasagna pan with cooking spray. Place ⅓ of the marinara sauce on the bottom of the pan. Cover with 3 noodles and ½ the ricotta cheese. Repeat. Top with marinara sauce.

Bake for 45 minutes in a 350 degree oven.

Yield: 1 lasagna

Nutrition Facts

Serving size: 1/6 of a recipe (6.1 ounces).

Amount Per Serving	
Calories	468.24
Calories From Fat (20%)	95.51
	% Daily Value
Total Fat 10.76g	**17%**
Saturated Fat 1.5g	**8%**
Cholesterol 0mg	**0%**
Sodium 215.91mg	**9%**
Potassium 363.29mg	**10%**
Total Carbohydrates 78.37g	**26%**
Fiber 3.45g	**14%**
Sugar 1.25g	
Protein 14.04g	**28%**

Black Bean Enchiladas

8 oz tomato sauce
½ cup water
⅛ tsp ground cumin
3 Tbsp picante sauce
1 ½ tsp chili powder
12 oz burger crumbles OR ground beef
1 tsp dry onion soup mix
½ cup low-sodium canned black beans, drained
¼ cup finely chopped onion
2 Tbsp chopped fresh cilantro
½ cup Vegan Cheese Sauce (see recipe)
6 Food for Life Sprouted Corn tortillas
½ bag grated cheese

Procedure

Stir the tomato sauce, water, cumin, salsa, and chili powder together in a medium saucepan. Heat through and simmer for 5 minutes.

Add the crumbles and heat for an additional 5 minutes.

Add onion soup mix, beans, onion, cilantro, and ¼ cup of cheese sauce. Mix well.

Preheat oven to 350°F.

Place the tortillas in a microwave for 15-20 seconds to soften.

Divide the filling and fill each tortilla, folding the tortilla underneath.

Pour cheese sauce on top of enchiladas.

Top with grated cheese.

Bake for 15 minutes until the cheese has melted and the enchiladas are heated through.

Yield: 6 servings

Nutrition Facts

Serving size: 1/6 of a recipe (9.3 ounces).

Amount Per Serving	
Calories	363.84
Calories From Fat (23%)	82.87
	% Daily Value
Total Fat 9.27g	**14%**
Saturated Fat 1.53g	**8%**
Cholesterol 0mg	**0%**
Sodium 1627.48mg	**68%**
Potassium 592.55mg	**17%**
Total Carbohydrates 37.36g	**12%**
Fiber 8.82g	35%
Sugar 3.91g	
Protein 33.1g	66%

Healthy Cheese Sauce

1 ¼ cups water
¼ cup raw cashew pieces
1 Tbsp nutritional yeast flakes
1 cup frozen, cooked brown rice
1 tsp salt
¼ tsp garlic powder
1 tsp onion powder
1 ½ Tbsp lemon juice

Procedure

Blend all the ingredients in a food processor or blender until creamy, about 5 minutes.

Yield: 8 Servings

Nutrition Facts

Serving size: 1/8 of a recipe (2.4 ounces).

Amount Per Serving	
Calories	37.8
Calories From Fat (13%)	4.98
	% Daily Value
Total Fat 0.59g	**<1%**
Saturated Fat 0.11g	**<1%**
Cholesterol 0mg	**0%**
Sodium 373.36mg	**16%**
Potassium 91.38mg	**3%**
Total Carbohydrates 6.82g	**2%**
Fiber 0.57g	**2%**
Sugar 0.25g	
Protein 1.41g	3%

Sesame Chik'n with Peanut Sauce

½	tsp	canola oil
2 ¼	tsp	toasted sesame oil
¼	cup	finely chopped onion
3		green onions, minced
1		clove garlic, minced
2	Tbsp	grated carrot
1 ½	cups	Quorn Chik'n chunks or chicken, cut into 1" chunks
1	Tbsp	low-sodium soy sauce
1 ½	tsp	Regular or vegan chicken broth
1	Tbsp	floral honey
	Pinch	cayenne pepper (optional)
8		large Romaine lettuce leaves
8	Tbsp	Thai peanut sauce (available in the international foods section of grocery stores. Check for low sugar content)

Procedure

Heat oils in a wok or large frying pan over medium heat.

Fry Quorn for 2-3 minutes until slightly brown. Add chopped onion, green onions, garlic, carrot, and sauté until the onion is tender, 3 to 4 minutes.

Stir in the remaining ingredients, except the lettuce and sauce, and stir fry for an additional 5 minutes.

Remove from the heat and allow to cool briefly before using.

Place ¼ cup on each lettuce leaf, drizzle with 1 Tbsp of peanut sauce.

Yield: 8 servings

Nutrition Facts

Serving size: 1/8 of a recipe (2.4 ounces).

Amount Per Serving	
Calories	100.43
Calories From Fat (58%)	58.16
	% Daily Value
Total Fat 6.85g	**11%**
Saturated Fat 1.2g	**6%**
Cholesterol 0mg	**0%**
Sodium 165.99mg	**7%**
Potassium 154.67mg	**4%**
Total Carbohydrates 6.76g	**2%**
Fiber 1.16g	**5%**
Sugar 2.95g	
Protein 4.54g	**9%**

Pasta Bake

6	oz	whole grain macaroni
½	cup	yellow onion
2		cloves garlic, minced
2	Tbsp	olive oil
1	cup	vegan burger crumbles OR ground beef
1	tsp	Italian seasoning
2	tsp	dried basil
1	jar	marinara sauce
½		can chopped tomatoes
½		medium zucchini, cut into ¾-inch cubes
2	Tbsp	chopped fresh parsley
¾	cup	ricotta cheese
1	pinch	cayenne pepper, or to taste
2	oz	mozzarella cheese
		Cooking spray

Procedure

Preheat oven to 350°F.

Spray an 8″ square baking dish with cooking spray.

Cook pasta according to package directions.

Sauté the onion and garlic in olive oil, 3 to 4 minutes. Add crumbles, Italian seasoning and ½ teaspoon of the basil, and sauté for 2 minutes. Stir in the marinara sauce, tomatoes, zucchini, and parsley, and let simmer for 15 to 20 minutes.

Mix ricotta, cayenne, and basil.

Place the pasta in the baking dish. Add half the filling to the pasta, and mix well. Spread the ricotta cheese mixture evenly over the pasta. Top with remaining sauce.

Bake for 25 minutes, until bubbly.

Servings: 8

Nutrition Facts

Serving size: 1/8 of a recipe (0.9 ounces).

Amount Per Serving	
Calories	12
Calories From Fat (48%)	5.76
	% Daily Value
Total Fat 0.65g	**<1%**
Saturated Fat 0.01g	**<1%**
Cholesterol 0mg	**0%**
Sodium 2.9mg	**<1%**
Potassium 61.63mg	**2%**
Total Carbohydrates 1.48g	**<1%**
Fiber 0.45g	**2%**
Sugar 0.25g	
Protein 0.35g	**<1%**

Baked Mini Egg Rolls & Hot Mustard Sauce

You're playing reactive hypoglycemia roulette if you purchase egg rolls from a Chinese restaurant. They are high in carbs and contain unknown amounts of sugar. These rolls are more balanced with edamame and peanuts providing protein. They don't have hidden sugars--but they taste like the real thing!

Egg Rolls

1 Tbsp soy sauce
1 tsp rice vinegar
2 tsp cornstarch
1 cup shredded cabbage
1 Tbsp sesame oil
½ cup shredded carrots
2 cloves garlic, minced
1 Tbsp minced fresh ginger
¼ cup sliced water chestnuts, drained and chopped
1 cup frozen, shelled edamame, thawed
2 Tbsp finely chopped roasted peanuts
26 won ton skins
1 large cage free egg, lightly beaten

Hot Mustard Sauce

2 Tbsp powdered yellow mustard
1 Tbsp water
1 tsp honey
1 tsp rice vinegar

Procedure

To make Egg Rolls:

Preheat oven to 425 degrees F.

Whisk soy sauce, vinegar and 1 tsp. cornstarch in a small bowl.

Stir fry cabbage and carrots in 1 teaspoon of sesame oil for 3 minutes.

Add garlic, ginger, water chestnuts, edamame, peanuts and oil. Stir for one minute until heated through.

Add soy sauce mixture to pan and stir until thickened.

Prepare a baking sheet by spraying with cooking spray.

Place 1Tbsp of the mixture in the center of a won ton wrap. Fold one corner over the filling followed by two side corners. Finally, roll into an egg roll shape.

Place egg roll on the baking sheet. Repeat for all egg rolls. Spray lightly over all rolls with cooking spray.

Turn rolls after 10 minutes.

While rolls are baking, place all mustard sauce ingredients into a small bowl and whisk together.

Yield: 26 rolls

Nutrition Facts

Serving size: 1 roll

Amount Per Serving	
Calories	116.8
Calories From Fat (14%)	16.4
	% Daily Value
Total Fat 1.87g	3%
Saturated Fat 0.32g	2%
Cholesterol 11.01mg	4%
Sodium 225.12mg	9%
Potassium 78.89mg	2%
Total Carbohydrates 20.49g	7%
Fiber 1.16g	5%
Sugar 0.65g	
Protein 4.35g	9%

Black Bean Chilaquiles

Short on time for dinner? These chilaquiles are healthful--and fast.

1	Tbsp	olive oil
2	cups	blue tortilla chips
½	cup	salsa
¼	cup	bell pepper, diced
½	can	black beans, drained and rinsed
1	Tbsp	cilantro, chopped
1		green onion, chopped
½		small tomato, chopped
½	ea	avocado (diced, for garnish)
1	cup	cabbage, shredded

Procedure

Sauté tortilla chips in olive oil for 1 minute.

Add salsa and peppers to pan, and stir well. Continue cooking until chips become slightly soggy.

Add remaining ingredients, reserving 1T of cilantro, scallions, tomato for garnish. Continue to sauté for 3-4 minutes until heated through.

Serve on a bed of cabbage. Garnish with chopped cilantro, scallions, fresh tomato, and avocado.

Nutrition Facts

Serving size: ½ recipe

Amount Per Serving	
Calories	668.94
Calories From Fat (28%)	189.51
	% Daily Value
Total Fat 21.82g	**34%**
Saturated Fat 3.12g	**16%**
Cholesterol 0mg	**0%**
Sodium 926.95mg	**39%**
Potassium 1130.66mg	**32%**
Total Carbohydrates 104.66g	**35%**
Fiber 16.09g	**64%**
Sugar 5.77g	
Protein 18.15g	**36%**

Black Bean Tostadas with Garlic Greens

These are best with homemade tortillas, as you can get the small size (5") that works best for tostadas.

2	Tbsp	olive oil, divided
4	10-inch	whole wheat tortillas
1	cup	diced red onion
1	can	black beans, drained and rinsed
2	tsp	smoked paprika
½	tsp	dried oregano
4	cloves	garlic, minced
1	head	spinach, rinsed and torn into bite-size pieces
½	ea	avocado (diced, for garnish)
1	cup	fresh salsa
4	Tbsp	chopped cilantro
4	Tbsp	sour cream

Procedure

Crisp tortillas by spraying a griddle with cooking spray and cooking each side for 1-2 minutes.

Saute onion until softened. Add beans, paprika, and oregano.

Reduce heat to low and simmer.

Meanwhile, saute garlic in remaining oil until lightly browned. Add the spinach and saute until wilted.

Assemble by spreading a generous spoonful of beans on each tostada.

Top with greens.

Garnish with remaining ingredients.

Yield: 4 tostadas

Nutrition Facts

Serving Size: 1 tostada

Amount Per Serving	
Calories	342.01
Calories From Fat (42%)	143.74
	% Daily Value
Total Fat 16.55g	**25%**
Saturated Fat 3.02g	**15%**
Cholesterol 5.85mg	**2%**
Sodium 763.18mg	**32%**
Potassium 1064.72mg	**30%**
Total Carbohydrates 41.14g	**14%**
Fiber 10.48g	**42%**
Sugar 4.45g	
Protein 11.29g	**23%**

General Tao's Chikin

This kicked-up dish tastes wonderful with steamed broccoli and brown rice (limit yourself to 1/3 cup of rice)

1	package	Quorn chickin chunks OR 1lb chicken, cut into chunks
1		egg
3/4	cup	cornstarch
4	Tbs	sesame oil
3		chopped green onions
1	Tbsp	minced ginger
1	Tbsp	minced garlic
2/3	cup	vegetable stock
2	Tbsp	soy sauce
3	Tbsp	fructose
		red pepper to taste
1	Tbsp	sherry, optional
1	Tbsp	cornstarch dissolved in 2 tablespoons water
1	Tbsp	white vinegar

Procedure

Whisk egg in a small bowl. Empty Quorn into the bowl and toss to coat.

Sprinkle 3/4 cup cornstarch over Quorn, toss to coat (do not overtoss.

Fry Quorn for 8 minutes, medium high heat in a wok. Push to one side.

Add green onions, ginger, garlic to the wok center, cook for 2 minutes.

Add vegetable stock, soy sauce, fructose, red pepper and vinegar.

Add cornstarch to the center and heat thoroughly until bubbling.

Push the Quorn to the center and mix well.

Servings: 4

Nutrition Facts

Serving size: ¼ recipe

Amount Per Serving	
Calories	515.36
Calories From Fat (35%)	182.24
	% Daily Value
Total Fat 20.48g	**32%**
Saturated Fat 2.62g	**13%**
Cholesterol 56.6mg	**19%**
Sodium 1036.27mg	**43%**
Potassium 399.19mg	**11%**
Total Carbohydrates 55.97g	**19%**
Fiber 6.24g	**25%**
Sugar 12.47g	
Protein 25.9g	**52%**

Indian Stuffed Peppers

The slow cooker will do all of the work for you in this dish. All you have to do for dinner is slice the tops from the peppers, remove the seeds, fill with the filling, and bake.

4		large red bell peppers
1	cup	chopped onion
2	tsp	yellow mustard
1	tsp	cumin seeds
1	tsp	ground coriander
½	tsp	salt
¼	tsp	cayenne pepper
2	cups	shredded green cabbage
1	cup	diced sweet potato
2	cups	cooked chickpeas
1	Tbsp	minced fresh ginger
3	cloves	garlic, minced (about 1 Tbs.)
¼	cup	vegetable broth
¼	cup	chopped cilantro
2	Tbsp	chopped roasted cashews
3/4	cup	plain yogurt
2 ½	Tbsp	prepared mango chutney

Procedure

Place onion, yellow mustard, cumin seeds, coriander, salt, cayenne pepper, cabbage, potato, chickpeas, ginger, garlic, and vegetable broth in a slow cooker. Cook for 6 hours.

When done, stir in in cilantro and cashews.

Slice tops off peppers and remove seeds. Fill with slow cooker filling and place caps on top.

Place peppers in a deep baking pan. Place ½" water in the pan and cover with foil.

Bake for 40 minutes at 375 degrees.

Combine yogurt and chutney. Drizzle over peppers to serve.

Servings: 4

Nutrition Facts

Serving size: ¼ recipe

Amount Per Serving	
Calories	337.31
Calories From Fat (14%)	48.8
	% Daily Value
Total Fat 5.57g	**9%**
Saturated Fat 1.17g	**6%**
Cholesterol 2.91mg	**<1%**
Sodium 979.53mg	**41%**
Potassium 956.91mg	**27%**
Total Carbohydrates 58.27g	**19%**
Fiber 12.88g	**52%**
Sugar 13.81g	
Protein 13.04g	**26%**

Jamaican Jerk Chili

So easy! Bung it all in the slow cooker...and enjoy hours later!

1 can kidney beans, drained and rinsed

1 can red beans, drained and rinsed

1 can diced tomatoes, 14.5oz

1 can tomato purée, 14.5oz

4 ea red potatoes, cut into bite-sized pieces

1 pkg vegetarian meat crumbles, 8oz OR 12 oz ground beef

1 large onion, chopped

2 Tbsp vinegar

2 Tbsp jerk seasoning (check for sugar content)

½ cup water

1 Tbsp fructose

¼-½ tsp minced Scotch bonnet or habanero chile, or to taste

Procedure

Combine all ingredients in 4-qt. slow cooker or large pot.

Stir in ½ cup water. Cook for 6-8 hours on low. Yield: 8

Nutrition Facts

Serving size: 1/8 recipe

Amount Per Serving	
Calories	219.18
Calories From Fat (5%)	10.61
	% Daily Value
Total Fat 1.23g	**2%**
Saturated Fat 0.23g	**1%**
Cholesterol 0mg	**0%**
Sodium 547.32mg	**23%**
Potassium 903.94mg	**26%**
Total Carbohydrates 42.16g	**14%**
Fiber 10.22g	**41%**
Sugar 7.17g	
Protein 11.75g	**24%**

Kidney Bean Burger

Use Ezekiel 4:9 buns for this burger (available in health food stores), and serve with a garden salad.

2 cans kidney beans, drained and rinsed well
1 onion
2 cloves garlic
3/4 cup whole wheat bread crumbs
1/8 cup whole wheat flour
1 Tbsp tomato paste
1 Tbsp cayenne pepper
1 ea egg
½ tsp oregano
½ tsp salt
1 spray olive oil

Procedure

Chop garlic and onion in a food processor. Add everything else and process until blended. Divide into 6 balls. Flatten into ½" patties.

Spray a frying pan with olive oil.

Cook on medium 4-5 minutes each side.

Yield: 6 burgers

Nutrition Facts

Serving size: 1 burger

Amount Per Serving	
Calories	219.58
Calories From Fat (7%)	15.98
	% Daily Value
Total Fat 1.86g	3%
Saturated Fat 0.55g	3%
Cholesterol 0.85mg	<1%
Sodium 548.3mg	23%
Potassium 533.9mg	15%
Total Carbohydrates 40.73g	14%
Fiber 10.38g	42%
Sugar 5.22g	
Protein 11.3g	23%

Mushroom Parcels

You'll want to save these for a special occasion, like a birthday or holiday dinner. Save a little time by purchasing the brown rice ready made from the frozen food section.

1	cup	cooked brown rice
1		onion, finely chopped
	cloves	garlic, crushed or finely chopped
1	jar	antipasto mushrooms, minus a tbsp mushrooms (make sure they are vegan), drain and reserve the oil.
1	cup	chestnut mushrooms, chopped
1	cup	portobello mushrooms, chopped
1	tsp	fresh oregano, minced
1	tsp	fresh basil, minced
1	cup	veggie burger crumbles, defrosted
1	tsp	fresh basil, chopped
1	Tbs	tomato puree
1		onion finely chopped
1	cup	rolled oats
½	cup	butter
1/8	tsp	pepper
1/8	tsp	salt
1/8	cup	water
1	tsp	mixed Italian herbs
8	ea	fresh basil leaves
2	Tbsp	tomato paste
1	recipe	whole wheat puff pastry (see Breads section for recipe) rolled into 4 x 8" squares

Procedure

Preheat oven to 390 degrees.

Sauté the onions and garlic in the reserved mushroom oil until soft. Add the rice, mushrooms, oregano and basil. Mix well.

Place veggie burger crumbles, remaining Tbsp mushrooms, tomato puree and basil in a food processor. Blend.

In a small bowl, mix onion, salt, pepper, oats, herbs and water. Split into 4 and form 4 sausage balls with hands.

Put a sheet of puff pastry on a clean surface. Spread with ½Tbsp tomato paste and top with 2 evenly spaced basil leaves. Repeat for other three pastry squares.

Spread the rice mix in the center of each pastry square in a strip. Top with the veggie crumble mix and finally the "sausage ball".

Fold up all four corners so that it forms a parcel. Brush with beaten egg.

Bake for 20-25 minutes until golden brown.

Yield: 6 servings

Nutrition Facts

Serving size: 1/6 recipe

Amount Per Serving	
Calories	429.13
Calories From Fat (38%)	161.42
	% Daily Value
Total Fat 18.45g	**28%**
Saturated Fat 10.25g	**51%**
Cholesterol 40.67mg	**14%**
Sodium 324.4mg	**14%**
Potassium 484.38mg	**14%**
Total Carbohydrates 54.84g	**18%**
Fiber 5.95g	**24%**
Sugar 4.03g	
Protein 12.7g	**25%**

Serving size: ¼ recipe

Amount Per Serving	
Calories	354.11
Calories From Fat (32%)	113.47
	% Daily Value
Total Fat 12.99g	**20%**
Saturated Fat 1.58g	**8%**
Cholesterol 0mg	**0%**
Sodium 530.75mg	**22%**
Potassium 242.26mg	**7%**
Total Carbohydrates 48.11g	**16%**
Fiber 2.88g	**12%**
Sugar 2.71g	
Protein 11.5g	**23%**

Supreme Burrito Pie

It's the refried beans that add the protein to this dish. Refried beans aren't actually fried--the Spanish word refrito means "twice cooked" but was mistakenly translated as "refried".

2	cans	refried beans
1	can	fresh salsa
1		tomato, diced
2	cups	shredded romaine heart lettuce
2	oz	sliced black olives
3	Tbsp	fresh cilantro coarsely chopped
4		whole wheat tortillas

Procedure

Place one tortilla on the bottom of a n 8"round casserole dish.

Spread ¼ of the refried beans and ¼ of the salsa on the tortilla.

Continue layering the tortilla, refried beans and salsa. Finish with a layer of beans and salsa.

Bake in the oven at 450 degrees for about 20 minutes.

Garnish with the remaining ingredients.

Yield: 8 servings

Nutrition Facts

Serving size: 1/8 recipe

Amount Per Serving	
Calories	131.96
Calories From Fat (19%)	25.51
	% Daily Value
Total Fat 2.92g	**4%**
Saturated Fat 0.72g	**4%**
Cholesterol 5.04mg	**2%**
Sodium 549.48mg	**23%**
Potassium 374.02mg	**11%**
Total Carbohydrates 21.67g	**7%**
Fiber 5.13g	**21%**
Sugar 2.05g	
Protein 5.69g	**11%**

Thai Chik'n Pizza

You can purchase tamarind from Indian or oriental grocery stores.

¼ cup peanut butter
1 Tbsp soy sauce
1 Tbsp chili paste
1 Tbsp fructose
2 ¼ tsp tamarind paste
1 clove garlic
½ tsp curry powder
¼ tsp sesame oil
¼ tsp grated fresh ginger
1 recipe wholewheat pizza dough (see Breads section for recipe)
4 white button mushrooms, thinly sliced
3/4 cup diced Quorn OR chicken
½ cup diced red bell pepper
1 ea small shallot, diced
1/3 cup chopped cilantro leaves for garnish

Procedure

Preheat oven to 425 degrees F.

Put peanut butter, tamari, soy sauce, fructose, tamarind, garlic, curry powder, oil, and ginger in blender. Blend until just creamy.

Sprinkle a pizza stone with corn flour and place the pizza dough on it.

Spread peanut butter mixture over dough.

Sprinkle with remaining ingredients.

Bake for 25 minutes.

Garnish with cilantro.

Servings: 8

Nutrition Facts

Serving size: 1/8 recipe

Amount Per Serving	
Calories	130.56
Calories From Fat (32%)	41.95
	% Daily Value
Total Fat 4.97g	**8%**
Saturated Fat 0.97g	**5%**
Cholesterol 0mg	**0%**
Sodium 188.51mg	**8%**
Potassium 305.1mg	**9%**
Total Carbohydrates 17.03g	**6%**
Fiber 1.39g	**6%**
Sugar 2.88g	
Protein 6.28g	**13%**

Lunch

Egg Salad Sandwich

2 free-range or cage-free eggs
1 Tbsp sour cream
2 tsp pickle relish
2 tsp mayonnaise
¼ tsp mustard
1 pinch salt
¼ cup celery chopped
2 slices whole-grain or sprouted-grain bread
1 pinch paprika

Procedure

Bring eggs to boil in pan of water. Boil for 10 minutes. Cool.

In a small bowl, mash all ingredients together.

Spread the mixture between two slices of whole-grain bread.

Yield: 1 full sandwich

Nutrition Facts

Serving size: ½ of a recipe.

Amount Per Serving	
Calories	148
Calories From Fat (41%)	60.15
	% Daily Value
Total Fat 7g	**11%**
Saturated Fat 2g	**10%**
Cholesterol 215mg	**72%**
Sodium 296mg	**12%**
Total Carbohydrates 14g	**5%**
Fiber 3g	**12%**
Protein 9g	**18%**

"Chikin" Salad with Ryvita crackers

This chicken-style spread is a no-cook dish that's ready in 5 minutes.

½	cup	raw sunflower seeds (soaked 3 hours)
½	cup	raw cashews (soaked 3 hours)
¼	cup	ground pecans
2	inch	piece of cucumber
1	Tbsp	onion
1		celery stick
1	tsp	dill
¼	tsp	curry powder
3	Tbs	lemon juice
½	tsp	salt
½	tsp	black pepper
1	ea	small carrot, chopped
8	ea	Ryvita whole grain crackers

Procedure

Place all ingredients into a blender and pulse for 2-3 minutes. Serve with Ryvita whole grain crackers. Yield: 4 servings

Nutrition Facts

Serving Size: ¼ recipe

Amount Per Serving	
Calories	328.35
Calories From Fat (54%)	177.4
	% Daily Value
Total Fat 21.19g	**33%**
Saturated Fat 2.87g	**14%**
Cholesterol 0mg	**0%**
Sodium 435.86mg	**18%**
Potassium 461.14mg	**13%**
Total Carbohydrates 30.89g	**10%**
Fiber 6.95g	**28%**
Sugar 3.44g	
Protein 8.4g	**17%**

Chilean Corn and "Turkey" Chowder

The slow cooker in my house is indispensable. Throw the ingredients on low at 7 am and it will be ready by lunchtime.

4 cups vegetable broth

1 rib celery with leaves, chopped

2 cloves garlic, minced (2 tsp.)

1 bay leaf

1 sprig whole thyme, plus 2 Tbs. chopped fresh thyme, divided

1 medium onion, peeled and diced (1 cup)

1 lb small white potatoes, diced (4 cups)

4 cups frozen corn kernels

2 cups chopped vegan turkey roast, or 3 frozen vegan chicken cutlets, thawed and chopped

¼ cup flour

4 plum tomatoes, peeled, seeded, and diced (for garnish)

1 medium avocado, diced (for garnish)

¼ cup coarsely chopped cilantro (for garnish)

2 Tbsp lime juice, plus lime wedges (for garnish)

Procedure

Place first 9 ingredients (up to the turkey roast) in a crock pot. Cook on low for 4-6 hours.

½ hour before serving, dissolve flour in ½ cup water. Add to crock pot and turn to high. Stir well.

Cook for 30 minutes on high.

Stir in tomatoes, avocado, cilantro, lime juice, cayenne pepper, lime wedges.

Yield: 8 servings

Nutrition Facts

Serving size: 1/8 recipe (about 16 oz)

Amount Per Serving	
Calories	375.29
Calories From Fat (20%)	75.22
	% Daily Value
Total Fat 8.64g	**13%**
Saturated Fat 1.36g	**7%**
Cholesterol 2.49mg	**<1%**
Sodium 1357.42mg	**57%**
Potassium 1152.58mg	**33%**
Total Carbohydrates 59.22g	**20%**
Fiber 10.35g	**41%**
Sugar 6.89g	
Protein 19.17g	**38%**

Curried Cauliflower Soup

This unusual dish has its roots in British and Indian cooking.

2 Tbsp olive oil

1 small onion, chopped (1 cup)

1 medium tart apple, such as Granny Smith, peeled, cored, and coarsely chopped (1 cup)

1 Tbsp curry powder

1 clove garlic, sliced (1 tsp.)

1 head cauliflower, chopped into 1-inch pieces (6 cups)

4 cups low-sodium vegetable broth

1 tsp honey or agave nectar

1 tsp rice wine vinegar

Procedure

Place all ingredients except for honey and vinegar into a crock pot.

Cook on low for 6 hours.

Blend ½ of the mixture in a blender and return to soup.

Stir in honey and vinegar just before serving. Yield: 6 servings

Nutrition Facts

Serving size: 1/6 recipe (8.2 oz)

Amount Per Serving	
Calories	180.12
Calories From Fat (36%)	64.01
	% Daily Value
Total Fat 7.28g	**11%**
Saturated Fat 1.25g	**6%**
Cholesterol 1.64mg	**<1%**
Sodium 1090.91mg	**45%**
Potassium 387.15mg	**11%**
Total Carbohydrates 25.6g	**9%**
Fiber 3.8g	**15%**
Sugar 4.65g	
Protein 4.75g	**10%**

Curried Seitan Salad Pita Pockets

If curried seitan sounds unusual to you...just wait until you taste it. It's reminiscent of curried turkey.

1/3 cup Vegenaise
2 Tbsp mango chutney
2 tsp curry powder
1 8-oz pkg. seitan, rinsed and drained
¼ cup frozen peas, thawed
3 Tbsp red onion
3 Tbsp salted roasted cashews
½ tsp pepper
¼ tsp salt
2 Tbsp currants
2 cups shredded romaine lettuce
4 thin slices tomato
4 rounds whole wheat pita halves

Procedure

Combine first 10 ingredients in a food processor. Chop until mixture resembles turkey salad. Place seitan salad, lettuce, and tomato in pita pockets. Yield: 4 pockets

Nutrition Facts

Serving size: ¼ recipe (6 ½ oz)

Amount Per Serving	
Calories	339.89
Calories From Fat (39%)	131.98
	% Daily Value
Total Fat 14.69g	**23%**
Saturated Fat 2.08g	**10%**
Cholesterol 7.56mg	**3%**
Sodium 943.89mg	**39%**
Potassium 429.66mg	**12%**
Total Carbohydrates 34.57g	**12%**
Fiber 7.32g	**29%**
Sugar 5.63g	
Protein 18.45g	**37%**

Easy Tuna Salad Recipe

Not tuna...but you'll think it is!

3/4 cup raw sunflower seeds (soaked for 8 hours)

½ cup raw almonds (soak for 8 hours)

2 stalks celery chopped

1 clove garlic minced

1 Tbsp lemon juice

½ tsp dry dill weed

1/8 tsp celery seed

1-2 Tbsp olive oil

Procedure

Place all ingredients in the food processor with the S blade and process until the mixture resembles tuna salad.

Yield: 4 servings

Nutrition Facts

Serving size: ¼ recipe (about 2½ oz)

Amount Per Serving	
Calories	257.65
Calories From Fat (75%)	192.49
	% Daily Value
Total Fat 22.82g	**35%**
Saturated Fat 2.09g	**10%**
Cholesterol 0mg	**0%**
Sodium 21.07mg	**<1%**
Potassium 324.31mg	**9%**
Total Carbohydrates 9.16g	**3%**
Fiber 4.12g	**16%**
Sugar 1.66g	
Protein 8.23g	**16%**

Garbanzo Croquettes

I grew up loving potato croquettes (a thing of the past with reactive hypoglycemia!). These protein-packed cakes are wonderful served with a green salad.

2 cans garbanzo beans, drained
½ cup wholegrain breadcrumbs
¼ cup olive oil
1 pinch black pepper
1 pinch salt
8 sun-dried tomatoes, drained and finely chopped
1 Tbsp ground coriander
1 Tbsp ground cumin
3 cloves garlic, minced
3 Tbsp fresh parsley, chopped
½ cup whole wheat flour
2 Tbsp canola oil for frying

Procedure

Place all ingredients except for the flour in a food processor and pulse until well mixed. Divide into 18 portions and roll into mini logs.

Place flour into a small bowl and dip croquettes into the flour.

Shallow fry croquettes in oil on medium heat until golden brown.

Yield: 6 servings

Nutrition Facts

Serving size: 6

Amount Per Serving	
Calories	306.31
Calories From Fat (46%)	140.37
	% Daily Value
Total Fat 15.99g	**25%**
Saturated Fat 1.91g	**10%**
Cholesterol 0mg	**0%**
Sodium 367.91mg	**15%**
Potassium 275.74mg	**8%**
Total Carbohydrates 35.05g	**12%**
Fiber 5.02g	**20%**
Sugar 0.64g	
Protein 6.89g	**14%**

Sonya's French Lentil Soup

I make enough of this delicious soup to freeze several portions.

1 large onion, diced
2 stalks celery, chopped
6 cloves garlic, smashed
2 bay leaves
1 Tbsp tomato paste
1 ½ cup red wine
16-oz dried lentils, sorted and rinsed
6 cups vegetable broth
2 Tbsp dried thyme or oregano
1 Tbsp Dijon mustard
pepper to taste
chopped spinach, frozen or fresh

Procedure

Place all ingredients in a slow cooker on low. Cook for 6 hours,

Yield: 8 servings

Nutrition Facts

Serving size: 1/8 recipe (about 10 oz)

Amount Per Serving	
Calories	306.31
Calories From Fat (46%)	140.37
	% Daily Value
Total Fat 15.99g	**25%**
Saturated Fat 1.91g	**10%**
Cholesterol 0mg	**0%**
Sodium 367.91mg	**15%**
Potassium 275.74mg	**8%**
Total Carbohydrates 35.05g	**12%**
Fiber 5.02g	**20%**
Sugar 0.64g	
Protein 6.89g	**14%**

Vegetable and Quorn Skewers with Rosemary-Dijon Vinaigrette

You'll find Quorn in the freezer section of most grocery stores. A distant cousin of the mushroom, it's packed with protein.

Rosemary-Dijon Vinaigrette

4 Tbsp sherry vinegar

4 Tbsp Dijon mustard

3 Tbsp small shallots, minced

2 Tbsp lemon juice

1 Tbsp grated lemon zest

2/3 cup olive oil

2 Tbsp chopped fresh rosemary

Vegetable Skewers

½ bag Quorn chickin chunks

2 small red potatoes, quartered and cooked

24 sugar snap peas

24 button mushrooms

1 red bell pepper, cut into 1-inch pieces

1 red onion, cut into 1-inch pieces

1 medium yellow squash, cut into 12 rounds

1 medium zucchini, cut into 12 rounds

Procedure

To make Rosemary-Dijon Vinaigrette:

Combine all ingredients in a small bowl and whisk together.

To make Vegetable Skewers:

Thread vegetables onto wooden skewers.

Place skewers into a baking dish.

Baste generously with the vinaigrette. Reserve ¼ of the vinaigrette.

Marinate overnight in the refrigerator.

Broil vegetables until just blackened, turning once.

Brush remaining vinaigrette over the vegetables. Yield: 6 servings

Nutrition Facts

Serving size: 1/6 recipe (about 18 oz)

Amount Per Serving	
Calories	580.45
Calories From Fat (39%)	229.07
	% Daily Value
Total Fat 26g	**40%**
Saturated Fat 3.61g	**18%**
Cholesterol 0.42mg	**<1%**
Sodium 154.05mg	**6%**
Potassium 1751.61mg	**50%**
Total Carbohydrates 72.77g	**24%**
Fiber 12.55g	**50%**
Sugar 6.52g	
Protein 21.25g	**43%**

Salads

Caesar Salad

6	cups	chopped romaine lettuce
½	cup	thinly sliced red onion
¼	cup	pitted black olives
1	cup	organic, vegan croutons
½	cup	Caesar Salad Dressing (see recipe)

Procedure

Place all ingredients except for croutons in a bowl and toss well. Add croutons, and serve.

Yield: 7 servings

Nutrition Facts

Serving size: 1/7 of a recipe (2.9 ounces).

Amount Per Serving	
Calories	106.32
Calories From Fat (86%)	91.42
	% Daily Value
Total Fat 10.35g	**16%**
Saturated Fat 1.56g	**8%**
Cholesterol 0.34mg	**<1%**
Sodium 226.94mg	**9%**
Potassium 125.5mg	**4%**
Total Carbohydrates 3.3g	**1%**
Fiber 1.37g	**5%**
Sugar 0.8g	
Protein 0.95g	**2%**

Caesar Salad Dressing

½	cup	Vegenaise
2	Tbsp	canola oil
2	Tbsp	fresh lemon juice
2	cloves	garlic, minced
2	Tbsp	nutritional yeast flakes
½	tsp	salt
¼	tsp	citric acid

Procedure

Combine all the ingredients in a small bowl and mix until smooth and creamy.

Yield: 7 servings

Nutrition Facts

Serving size: 1/8 of a recipe (1 oz).

Amount Per Serving	
Calories	80.03
Calories From Fat (84%)	67.01
	% Daily Value
Total Fat 7.57g	**12%**
Saturated Fat 0.72g	**4%**
Cholesterol 5.04mg	**2%**
Sodium 378.1mg	**16%**
Potassium 126.17mg	**4%**
Total Carbohydrates 2.09g	**<1%**
Fiber 0.17g	**<1%**
Sugar 0.1g	
Protein 1.31g	3%

Dill and Cucumber Salad

2	cups	½-inch cucumber cubes
1	cup	½-inch tomato pieces
¼	cup	¼-inch red onion pieces
½	tsp	dried dill weed
⅛	tsp	salt
⅛	tsp	garlic powder
½	cup	sour cream

Procedure

Stir the celery seed, dill weed, salt, garlic powder and sour cream together. Add vegetables and toss.

Yield: 7 Servings

Nutrition Facts

Serving size: 1/7 of a recipe (2.3 oz).

Amount Per Serving	
Calories	11.06
Calories From Fat (10%)	1.08
	% Daily Value
Total Fat 0.13g	**<1%**
Saturated Fat 0.01g	**<1%**
Cholesterol 0mg	**0%**
Sodium 43.85mg	**2%**
Potassium 109.58mg	**3%**
Total Carbohydrates 2.26g	**<1%**
Fiber 0.65g	3%
Sugar 1.15g	
Protein 0.51g	**1%**

Black Bean-Avocado Salad

This makes a great side dish to a breaded chicken-style patty.

2 tbsp lemon juice
1 tbsp whole-grain mustard
1/8 tsp black pepper
1 pinch salt
2 tbsp olive oil
2 ea Roma tomatoes, chopped
1 can canned black beans, rinsed and drained
1 cup fresh or frozen corn, thawed
1 avocado, diced
½ cup diced sweet red pepper
½ cup coarsely chopped cilantro
¼ cup diced celery
2 green onions, trimmed and thinly sliced (about ¼ cup)

Procedure

Whisk together lemon juice, mustard, and olive oil in large bowl.

Add all remaining ingredients, and gently toss to combine. Yield: 4 servings.

Nutrition Facts

Serving size: ¼ recipe (about 9 oz)

Amount Per Serving	
Calories	341.06
Calories From Fat (36%)	121.92
	% Daily Value
Total Fat 14.24g	**22%**
Saturated Fat 1.95g	**10%**
Cholesterol 0mg	**0%**
Sodium 247.51mg	**10%**
Potassium 696.28mg	**20%**
Total Carbohydrates 49.37g	**16%**
Fiber 8.86g	**35%**
Sugar 3.48g	
Protein 6.28g	**13%**

Bok Choy Salad

2 ea Quorn breaded chikin patties, cooked and chopped into ¼" squares
½ cup olive oil
¼ cup white vinegar
¼ cup fructose
3 tbsp soy sauce
2 bunch baby bok choy, sliced
1 bunch green onions, chopped
½ cup slivered almonds, toasted
½ cup chow mein noodles

Procedure

Mix olive oil, white vinegar, fructose, and soy sauce in a large bowl.

Combine all ingredients in a large bowl and mix well.

Yield: 4 servings

Nutrition Facts

Serving size: ¼ recipe

Amount Per Serving	
Calories	655.96
Calories From Fat (57%)	375.37
	% Daily Value
Total Fat 43.04g	**66%**
Saturated Fat 5.42g	**27%**
Cholesterol 2.52mg	**<1%**
Sodium 1143.98mg	**48%**
Potassium 587.03mg	**17%**
Total Carbohydrates 43.52g	**15%**
Fiber 9.67g	39%
Sugar 17.41g	
Protein 28.37g	57%

Brit-Asian Salad

1	head	romaine lettuce (shredded)
1		tomato (diced)
1		avocado (diced)
½		cucumber (diced)
3	tbsp	onion (diced)
4	tbsp	sunflower seeds
2	tbsp	agave nectar
3	tbsp	lemon juice
¼	cup	Chinese fried wonton strips
¼	cup	cashews, toasted
1	ea	nori sheet, cut into very thin strips
		sea salt to taste

Procedure

Combine all ingredients into a large bowl. Mix well. Chill for 30 minutes.

Before serving, mix again for 2-3 minutes to blend flavors and soften the nori. Yield: 4 servings

Nutrition Facts

Serving size: ¼ recipe (about 11 oz)

Amount Per Serving	
Calories	210.71
Calories From Fat (48%)	101.21
	% Daily Value
Total Fat 12.08g	**19%**
Saturated Fat 1.56g	**8%**
Cholesterol 0.18mg	**<1%**
Sodium 112.27mg	**5%**
Potassium 852.78mg	**24%**
Total Carbohydrates 25.26g	**8%**
Fiber 7.95g	**32%**
Sugar 12.97g	
Protein 5.57g	**11%**

Chinese Chicken Salad

If you can't find spicy chicken-style patties, use plain instead.

4 cups romaine lettuce (shredded)

3-oz spicy breaded veggie chicken patty, cooked and sliced

2 stalks green onions, chopped

16 ea grape tomatoes

Dressing

2 tbsp olive oil

1 ½ tbsp rice wine vinegar

1 tbsp fructose

½ tsp salt

½ tsp Chinese 5-spice

Toasted sesame seeds (for garnish)

Procedure

Mix the salad ingredients together in a bowl.

Whisk the dressing ingredients together.

Combine and serve immediately. Yield: 2 servings

Nutrition Facts

Serving size: ½ recipe (about 20 oz)

Amount Per Serving	
Calories	488.48
Calories From Fat (42%)	202.93
	% Daily Value
Total Fat 23.95g	**37%**
Saturated Fat 3.34g	**17%**
Cholesterol 2.52mg	**<1%**
Sodium 1273.98mg	**53%**
Potassium 1373.17mg	**39%**
Total Carbohydrates 49.29g	**16%**
Fiber 13.75g	**55%**
Sugar 16.56g	
Protein 28.77g	**58%**

Christmas Salad

4 ea hard boiled, cage free eggs, peeled and sliced

1 ea Romaine lettuce, torn into small chunks

1 ea red leaf lettuce, torn into small chunks

1 heads Belgian endive, turn into small chunck

½ ea English cucumber, chopped

1 ea red bell pepper, chopped

1 ½ cup cherry tomatoes cut into quarters

1 ½ cup white mushrooms, sliced

1/8 cup balsamic vinegar

1/8 cup olive oil

¼ tsp ground black pepper

1 pinch salt

Procedure

Toss all ingredients together in a large bowl and serve immediately.

Yield: 12 servings

Nutrition Facts

Serving size: 1/12 recipe (about 7 oz)

Amount Per Serving	
Calories	78.59
Calories From Fat (49%)	38.54
	% Daily Value
Total Fat 4.35g	**7%**
Saturated Fat 0.88g	**4%**
Cholesterol 70.5mg	**24%**
Sodium 72.01mg	**3%**
Potassium 453.97mg	**13%**
Total Carbohydrates 6.58g	**2%**
Fiber 3.37g	**13%**
Sugar 1.96g	
Protein 4.27g	**9%**

Cranberry Spinach Salad

1 tbsp butter
3/4 cup almonds, blanched and slivered
1 lb spinach, rinsed and torn into bite-size pieces
1 cup dried cranberries
2 tbsp toasted sesame seeds
1 tbsp poppy seeds
1/3 cup fructose
2 tsp minced onion
¼ tsp paprika
¼ cup white wine vinegar
¼ cup cider vinegar
1 Tbsp garlic clove, minced
½ cup olive oil

Procedure

Saute almonds in butter for 2-3 minutes. In a medium bowl, whisk remaining ingredients. Serve immediately. Yield: 8 servings

Nutrition Facts

Serving size: 1/8 recipe (about 7 oz)

Amount Per Serving	
Calories	533.94
Calories From Fat (40%)	215.93
	% Daily Value
Total Fat 24.91g	**38%**
Saturated Fat 2.69g	**13%**
Cholesterol 3.82mg	**1%**
Sodium 49.11mg	**2%**
Potassium 489.52mg	**14%**
Total Carbohydrates 75.7g	**25%**
Fiber 8.07g	**32%**
Sugar 9.51g	
Protein 5.21g	**10%**

Dandelion and Bitter Greens Salad

4 tbsp chopped fresh tarragon
4 cloves garlic, minced (2 tsp.)
1 cup lemon juice
½ cup olive oil
1 bag Quorn chickin chunks
2 cups dandelion greens, thick stems trimmed
2 cups chicory leaves, outer ribs discarded, leaves torn into 2-inch pieces
2 cups baby arugula
1 medium Belgian endive, sliced into ½-inch-thick rings (1 cup)
1 medium carrot, grated (½ cup)
1 small fennel bulb, thinly sliced (½ cup)
¼ cup thinly sliced celery
¼ cup chopped parsley
Dash cayenne pepper

Procedure

Place tarragon, lemon juice, olive oil and garlic in a bowl. Whisk together.

Place ½ of the dressing in a Ziplock bag. Add the Quorn and shake well.

Cook the Quorn in a non-stick pan for 10 minutes until heated through.

Combine Quorn, dandelion greens, chicory, arugula, endive, carrot, fennel, celery, and parsley in large bowl.

Pour the remaining dressing on top and mix well.

Serve immediately.

Yield: 4 servings

Nutrition Facts

Serving size: ¼ recipe

Amount Per Serving	
Calories	435.21
Calories From Fat (63%)	272.57
	% Daily Value
Total Fat 30.84g	**47%**
Saturated Fat 4.28g	**21%**
Cholesterol 1.26mg	**<1%**
Sodium 538.22mg	**22%**
Potassium 1086mg	**31%**
Total Carbohydrates 29.22g	**10%**
Fiber 10.93g	**44%**
Sugar 4.83g	
Protein 16.21g	**32%**

Fall Salad

Make sure you use the plain chicken strips in the salad, and not the Italian ones, which lend too much of a strong flavor.

Lemon Dressing

¼ cup lemon juice

¼ cup olive oil

½ tsp salt

½ tsp cracked black pepper

½ tsp ground fennel seed

1 Tbsp cider vinegar

Salad

1 can beets (plain, in water)

1 fennel bulb (1 lb.)

6 oranges

6 cups watercress or mixed field greens (6oz.), coarsely chopped

1 head radicchio (4 oz.), thinly sliced

½ small red onion, thinly sliced (¼ cup)

2 cups Morningstar Farm Chicken Strips, cooked

16 pitted kalamata olives, halved

Procedure

To make Lemon Dressing:

Combine lemon dressing ingredients in a small bowl and mix well.

To make Salad:

Toss lemon dressing with salad ingredients.

Yield: 8 servings

Nutrition Facts

Serving size: 1/8 recipe (about 9 oz)

Amount Per Serving	
Calories	366.87
Calories From Fat (64%)	233.08
	% Daily Value
Total Fat 27.32g	**42%**
Saturated Fat 2.37g	**12%**
Cholesterol 0mg	**0%**
Sodium 285.69mg	**12%**
Potassium 666.68mg	**19%**
Total Carbohydrates 26.68g	**9%**
Fiber 8.37g	**33%**
Sugar 15.56g	
Protein 10g	**20%**

Fruit and Nut Salad

1 cup slivered almonds
1/3 cup fructose
½ cup olive oil
¼ cup distilled white vinegar
1 pinch salt and pepper, each
½ head iceberg lettuce, chopped
½ head romaine lettuce, chopped
1 cup chopped celery
¼ cup chopped fresh chives
½ cup dried, unsweetened cranberries
¼ cup mandarin orange segments (in juice, not syrup), drained
¼ cup sliced fresh peaches
¼ cup chopped fresh strawberries

Procedure

Combine almonds and fructose in a frying pan. Cook over medium heat until almonds are coated and fructose begins to brown. Remove almonds with a slotted spoon.

Mix the olive oil, vinegar, 2 tablespoons fructose, salt, and pepper in a small bowl.

Mix all ingredients together in a large bowl. Toss well and serve.

Yield: 8 servings

Nutrition Facts

Serving size: 1/8 recipe (about 5 oz)

Amount Per Serving	
Calories	395.47
Calories From Fat (51%)	201.34
	% Daily Value
Total Fat 23.3g	**36%**
Saturated Fat 2.58g	**13%**
Cholesterol 0mg	**0%**
Sodium 57.34mg	**2%**
Potassium 272.39mg	**8%**
Total Carbohydrates 45.32g	**15%**
Fiber 5.28g	**21%**
Sugar 11.04g	
Protein 4.42g	9%

Green Pepper Tomato Salad

This tangy salad can be served as a side dish. Serve on a bed of lettuce for a full meal.

3		medium tomatoes, seeded and chopped
1		medium green pepper, chopped
1		celery rib, thinly sliced
1	cup	chick peas, drained and rinsed
½	cup	chopped red onion
2	tbsp	cider vinegar
1	tbsp	fructose
½	tsp	salt
1/8	tsp	pepper

Procedure

Combine first five ingredients in a bowl.

Mix last four ingredients in a small bowl.

Combine all ingredients. Chill in refrigerator for 1 hour before serving.

Yield: 6 servings

Nutrition Facts

Serving size: 1/6 recipe (about 6 oz)

Amount Per Serving	
Calories	79.64
Calories From Fat (7%)	5.62
	% Daily Value
Total Fat 0.67g	**1%**
Saturated Fat 0.09g	**<1%**
Cholesterol 0mg	**0%**
Sodium 324.12mg	**14%**
Potassium 295.01mg	**8%**
Total Carbohydrates 16.24g	**5%**
Fiber 3.33g	**13%**
Sugar 4.61g	
Protein 2.98g	**6%**

Lettuce, Pomegranates and Pine Nuts Salad

½	cup	cashews, roasted
3	tbsp	pine nuts
2	cups	baby spinach
5	cups	romaine lettuce, torn
1	ea	garlic clove, thinly sliced
½	tbsp	olive oil
½		avocado, cored
¼	cup	Pomegranate seeds
2	tbsp	Lemon juice
1	pinch	salt

Procedure

Combine all ingredients in a large bowl and toss well.

Yield: 4 servings

Nutrition Facts

Serving size: ¼ recipe (about 5 oz)

Amount Per Serving	
Calories	214.28
Calories From Fat (69%)	147.71
	% Daily Value
Total Fat 17.55g	**27%**
Saturated Fat 2.59g	**13%**
Cholesterol 0mg	**0%**
Sodium 66mg	**3%**
Potassium 476.61mg	**14%**
Total Carbohydrates 12.83g	**4%**
Fiber 3.62g	**14%**
Sugar 3g	
Protein 5.23g	**10%**

Mexican Cucumber Salad

1	can	black beans
1		medium cucumber, chopped
1	can	whole kernel corn, drained
4	ea	Roma tomatoes, chopped
1		green bell pepper, chopped
1		red bell pepper, chopped
2	tbsp	red wine vinegar
1	tbsp	crushed red pepper flakes
½	tsp	garlic, minced
½	tsp	cumin
¼	tsp	dried cilantro
¼	tsp	salt
1/8	tsp	ground black pepper

Procedure

Combine all ingredients in a bowl and mix well.

Cover, and chill at least 1 hour before serving. Yield: 6 servings

Nutrition Facts

Serving size: 1/6 recipe

Amount Per Serving	
Calories	101.65
Calories From Fat (7%)	6.94
	% Daily Value
Total Fat 0.82g	**1%**
Saturated Fat 0.12g	**<1%**
Cholesterol 0mg	**0%**
Sodium 241.32mg	**10%**
Potassium 620.47mg	**18%**
Total Carbohydrates 20.51g	**7%**
Fiber 5.91g	**24%**
Sugar 6.31g	
Protein 5.1g	**10%**

Simple Chickpea Salad

1	can	chickpeas, drained
1 ½	cups	celery, diced
½	cup	vegan mayonnaise
2	Tbsp	lemon juice
4	ea	Roma tomatoes
2	Tbs	parsley
1	tsp	garlic powder
1	tsp	onion powder
		Salt and pepper, to taste
4	ea	wholegrain pita to serve

Procedure

Combine all ingredients. Chill for at least 30 minutes before serving.

Serve with fresh pita.

Yield: 8 servings

Nutrition Facts

Serving size: 1/8 recipe (about 6 oz)

Amount Per Serving	
Calories	183.88
Calories From Fat (28%)	51.89
	% Daily Value
Total Fat 5.92g	**9%**
Saturated Fat 0.71g	**4%**
Cholesterol 5.67mg	**2%**
Sodium 397.55mg	**17%**
Potassium 328.51mg	**9%**
Total Carbohydrates 29.45g	**10%**
Fiber 4.88g	**20%**
Sugar 2.58g	
Protein 5.45g	**11%**

Trinity Kale Salad

8 leaves each of curly kale, russian kale and dino kale (shredded)
1 cup cherry tomatoes halved
4 ea hard boiled eggs, diced
1 tomato (diced)
1 avocado (diced)
3 tbsp onion (diced)
2-3 tbsp olive oil
2 tbsp agave nectar
4 tbsp lemon juice
sea salt to taste

Procedure

Combine olive oil, lemon juice, salt and agave in the bottom of a large bowl. Whisk well.

Combine all other ingredients in the bowl. Mix well.

Chill for 2 hours before serving.

Yield: 4 servings

Nutrition Facts

Serving size: ¼ recipe

Amount Per Serving	
Calories	380.03
Calories From Fat (58%)	219.41
	% Daily Value
Total Fat 24.86g	**38%**
Saturated Fat 5.87g	**29%**
Cholesterol 576.64mg	**192%**
Sodium 244.4mg	**10%**
Potassium 743.04mg	**21%**
Total Carbohydrates 21.84g	**7%**
Fiber 4.54g	**18%**
Sugar 11.85g	
Protein 19.69g	39%

Sides

Amora's Salsa

2 large fresh tomatoes, whole and unpeeled
1 can Roma tomatoes, chopped
1 Tbsp canned green chilies
2 Tbsp diced red onion
3 Tbsp finely chopped fresh cilantro
¾ tsp salt
1 Tbsp lime juice

Procedure

Place all ingredients in a blender and blend for 30 seconds. Serve with baked, whole grain tortilla chips.

Yield: 14 servings

Nutrition Facts

Serving size: 1/14 of a recipe (0.8 ounces).

Amount Per Serving	
Calories	4.81
Calories From Fat (10%)	0.47
	% Daily Value
Total Fat 0.06g	**<1%**
Saturated Fat 0.01g	**<1%**
Cholesterol 0mg	**0%**
Sodium 125.99mg	**5%**
Potassium 55.66mg	**2%**
Total Carbohydrates 1.04g	**<1%**
Fiber 0.33g	**1%**
Sugar 0.64g	
Protein 0.23g	**<1%**

Pete's Guacamole

2		ripe avocados
1		plum tomato, chopped, small
2	tsp	fresh lime juice
½	tsp	salt
¼	tsp	garlic powder
¼	cup	chopped yellow onion
2	Tbsp	fresh chopped cilantro
2	tsp	minced jalapeno or Serrano chilies

Procedure

Mash avocado flesh in a bowl. Add remaining ingredients and stir well.

Yield: 12 servings

Nutrition Facts

Serving size: 1/12 of a recipe (1.2 ounces).

Amount Per Serving	
Calories	49.88
Calories From Fat (75%)	37.32
	% Daily Value
Total Fat 4.45g	**7%**
Saturated Fat 0.61g	**3%**
Cholesterol 0mg	**0%**
Sodium 99.68mg	**4%**
Potassium 155.04mg	**4%**
Total Carbohydrates 2.89g	**<1%**
Fiber 2.04g	**8%**
Sugar 0.25g	
Protein 0.62g	**1%**

Avocado Dip

Serve this dip with carrot chips and blue corn chips. Be careful with portions--you should eat more dip than chips!

2 avocados - peeled, pitted and diced

1 can black beans, drained and rinsed

1 can whole kernel corn, drained

1 ea medium onion, minced

3/4 cup salsa

1 tbsp chopped fresh cilantro

1 tbsp fresh lemon juice

½ tsp cumin

2 tbsp chili powder

1 pinch ground black pepper

1 pinch salt

Procedure

Place all ingredients into a food processor and process until just blended.

Yield: 12 servings

Nutrition Facts

Serving size: 1/12 recipe (3 oz)

Amount Per Serving	
Calories	91.16
Calories From Fat (45%)	40.96
	% Daily Value
Total Fat 4.88g	**8%**
Saturated Fat 0.69g	**3%**
Cholesterol 0mg	**0%**
Sodium 180.42mg	**8%**
Potassium 321.9mg	**9%**
Total Carbohydrates 11.31g	**4%**
Fiber 4.44g	**18%**
Sugar 1.56g	
Protein 2.73g	**5%**

Butternut Squash with Whole Wheat, Wild Rice & Onion Stuffing

This makes an excellent side dish for a serving of protein (e.g. Quorn).

4 medium-small butternut squashes (about 1pound each)
¾ cup brown rice (cooked)
1 Tbsp olive oil
1 cup chopped onion
1 clove garlic, minced
2 slices finely torn whole wheat bread
1 Tbsp sesame seeds
½ tsp thyme
½ tsp marjoram
½ tsp seasoned salt
1 cup fresh orange juice

Procedure

Cut the squashes in half and scoop out seeds and fibers.

Place cut side up on a baking sheet and bake for 45 minutes.

Remove from oven to cool slightly. Reduce oven temperature to 350°.

Saute onion and garlic until golden. Add all remaining ingredients to pan and mix well, ensuring rice is heated through (if cold).

Scoop out most of the pulp from the squashed evenly, leaving a "boat" with a ¼" thick shell.

Chop the squash into ¼" pieces. Stir into rice mixture.

Place squash and rice mixture back into the shells. Cover with foil and bake for 15 minutes until heated through.

Yield: 8 servings

Nutrition Facts

Serving size: 1/8 recipe (about 7 oz)

Amount Per Serving	
Calories	138.5
Calories From Fat (30%)	41.45
	% Daily Value
Total Fat 4.93g	**8%**
Saturated Fat 0.72g	**4%**
Cholesterol 0mg	**0%**
Sodium 181.78mg	**8%**
Potassium 540.85mg	**15%**
Total Carbohydrates 20.6g	**7%**
Fiber 7.75g	**31%**
Sugar 3.68g	
Protein 5.54g	**11%**

Five Pepper Hummus

Hummus should be a staple in any reactive hypoglycemic diet--it's packed with protein and is relatively low in calories.

1 large green bell pepper, seeded and chopped

1 can garbanzo beans, drained, 15oz

4 fresh jalapeno peppers, seeded

½ tsp citric acid

½ tsp cumin

1 jar banana peppers, drained, 16oz

1 clove garlic

1 tbsp ground cayenne pepper

2 tbsp ground black pepper

¼ cup tahini

Procedure

Place all ingredients into a food processor. Process until blended.

Serve with whole wheat pita bread or carrot chips.

Yield: 16 servings

Nutrition Facts

Serving size: 1/16 recipe

Amount Per Serving	
Calories	48.85
Calories From Fat (37%)	17.85
	% Daily Value
Total Fat 2.13g	**3%**
Saturated Fat 0.3g	**2%**
Cholesterol 0mg	**0%**
Sodium 48.76mg	**2%**
Potassium 108.04mg	**3%**
Total Carbohydrates 6.53g	**2%**
Fiber 1.68g	**7%**
Sugar 0.38g	
Protein 1.8g	**4%**

Fruit Salsa with Cinnamon Chips

This truly is a side dish: serve ½ a cup of the salsa and one tortilla with a large amount of protein such as a Quorn Chik'n cutlet.

2 kiwis, peeled and diced into ¼" cubes

2 Golden Delicious apples, peeled, diced into ¼" cubes

8-oz raspberries, quartered

1 lb strawberries, diced into ¼" cubes

2 tbsp fructose

3 tbsp 100% fruit preserves

10 whole wheat tortillas

butter flavored cooking spray

1/3 cup fructose

2 tsp cinnamon

Procedure

In a large bowl, thoroughly mix kiwis, Golden Delicious apples, raspberries, strawberries, 2T fructose and 100% fruit preserves.

Cover and place in the fridge.

Spray each tortilla with cooking spray. Keep in a stack.

Cut into wedges and place into a large Ziplock bag.

Pour fructose and cinnamon into the bag, shaking as you pour to evenly distribute. Close bag and shake well.

Bake for 10 minutes.

Allow to cool slightly. Serve with fruit.

Yield: 10 servings

Nutrition Facts

Serving size: 1/10 recipe (about 7 oz)

Amount Per Serving	
Calories	353.88
Calories From Fat (7%)	25.44
	% Daily Value
Total Fat 2.91g	**4%**
Saturated Fat 0.63g	**3%**
Cholesterol 0mg	**0%**
Sodium 206.84mg	**9%**
Potassium 229.49mg	**7%**
Total Carbohydrates 81.17g	**27%**
Fiber 3.97g	**16%**
Sugar 59.93g	
Protein 3.41g	**7%**

Greek-Mexican Couscous Salad

A true fusion dish! Try this fun recipe as a side to falafel or bean burritos (or, for an unusual combination--both!)

½ tsp ground cumin

½ tsp salt

1 tsp garlic clove, minced

1 cup whole-wheat couscous, cooked

1 can black beans, drained and rinsed

1 cup frozen corn kernels, thawed

½ cup chopped red onion

¼ cup cilantro, chopped

1 small jalapeño pepper, seeded and diced, optional

3 tbsp fresh lime juice

2 tbsp olive oil

Procedure

Mix all ingredients into a large bowl. Serve immediately or chill for 1 hour before serving. Yield: 4 servings

Nutrition Facts

Serving size: ¼ recipe (about 6 oz)

Amount Per Serving	
Calories	433.55
Calories From Fat (16%)	71.21
	% Daily Value
Total Fat 8.13g	**13%**
Saturated Fat 1.2g	**6%**
Cholesterol 0mg	**0%**
Sodium 400.93mg	**17%**
Potassium 929.89mg	**27%**
Total Carbohydrates 74.6g	**25%**
Fiber 11.11g	**44%**
Sugar 2.62g	
Protein 17.49g	35%

Mint Tabouleh

1 cup of cooked bulgur has 6g of protein, making this a nicely balanced dish you can also chow down on as a snack.

1 cup bulgur
3 Tbsp lemon juice
¼ tsp honey
3/4 cup finely chopped pistachios
1 cup finely chopped curly parsley
1 small English cucumber, finely chopped (1 cup)
1 medium tomato, finely chopped (1/3 cup)
4 green onions, finely chopped (1/3 cup)
1/3 cup finely chopped fresh mint
3 Tbsp lemon juice
3 tbsp olive oil

Procedure

Cook bulgur according to package instructions--adding 3 tablespoons of lemon and 3 tablespoons of honey to the water. When bulgur is cooked, add remaining ingredients and mix well. Yield: 6 servings

Nutrition Facts

Serving size: 1/6 recipe (about 6 oz)

Amount Per Serving	
Calories	195.53
Calories From Fat (62%)	121.43
	% Daily Value
Total Fat 14.13g	**22%**
Saturated Fat 1.83g	**9%**
Cholesterol 0mg	**0%**
Sodium 13.22mg	**<1%**
Potassium 415.92mg	**12%**
Total Carbohydrates 15.05g	**5%**
Fiber 4.36g	**17%**
Sugar 3.47g	
Protein 5.32g	**11%**

Spinach and Artichoke Dip

The best accompaniment for this dip would be raw corn chips from your local health food store. These can also be found online. An alternative would be to serve with a selection of dipping veggies.

1 can artichokes, chopped into ¼" chunks

1 cup cooked spinach, chopped into 14" pieces

1 cup Vegenaise

1 cup Parmesan cheese

½ tsp garlic clove, minced

½ tsp garlic powder

1 dash hot sauce

1 pinch pepper

1 pinch salt

Procedure

Add all ingredients to a large bowl. Mix well.

Yield: 10 servings

Nutrition Facts

Serving size: 1/10 recipe (about 2 oz)

Amount Per Serving	
Calories	121.51
Calories From Fat (74%)	90.23
	% Daily Value
Total Fat 10.2g	**16%**
Saturated Fat 2.56g	**13%**
Cholesterol 17.87mg	**6%**
Sodium 295.16mg	**12%**
Potassium 70.53mg	**2%**
Total Carbohydrates 3.6g	**1%**
Fiber 0.64g	3%
Sugar 0.14g	
Protein 4.32g	9%

Vegetable Pakoras

These are a tasty addition to an Indian dish (such as a dal or curry). I use a Fry Daddy to fry veggies. With an old-fashioned pan, heat the oil to 375°.

1 cup besan
½ tsp ground coriander
¼ tsp salt
1 tsp ground turmeric
½ tsp chili powder
½ tsp garam masala
2 cloves garlic, minced
¾ cup water
1 quart olive oil
4 cups vegetables: cauliflower, green beans, mushrooms, onion rings, slices of sweet potato, ¾" carrot chunks

Procedure

Warm oil while preparing vegetables (if not already prepared)

In a large bowl, combine the besan, coriander, salt, turmeric, chili powder, garam masala, garlic, and water.

Mix well to form a smooth batter. Toss the vegetables into the batter and mix well, evenly coat vegetables.

Fry for 3-4 minutes until golden brown.

Drain on paper towels before serving.

Amount Per Serving	
Calories	1594.21
Calories From Fat (82%)	1302.77
	% Daily Value
Total Fat 147.47g	**227%**
Saturated Fat 14.98g	**75%**
Cholesterol 0mg	**0%**
Sodium 405.03mg	**17%**
Potassium 3129.41mg	**89%**
Total Carbohydrates 61.81g	**21%**
Fiber 26.51g	**106%**
Sugar 25.29g	
Protein 23.05g	**46%**

Yield: 4 cups

Nutrition Facts

Serving size: 2/3 cup

Zucchini Cakes

These make a great side dish to any protein.

2 ½	cups	grated zucchini
1		egg, beaten
2	Tbsp	butter, melted
1	cup	bread crumbs
¼	cup	minced onion
1	tsp	Italian seasoning
¼	cup	whole wheat flour
½	cup	olive oil for frying

Procedure

Combine zucchini, egg, butter, seasoned crumbs, minced onion, and seasoning.

Shape mixture into 10 rounds. Flatten into patties then dredge in flour.

Heat oil over medium high heat in a skillet.

Fry patties 3 minutes each side until golden brown.

Yield: 5 servings (10 patties)

Nutrition Facts

Serving size: 2 patties (about 5 oz)

Note: nutritional information is for entire ½ cup olive oil used for frying. Depending on the heat setting of your pan, you may use less oil.

Amount Per Serving	
Calories	370.65
Calories From Fat (68%)	253.86
	% Daily Value
Total Fat 28.73g	**44%**
Saturated Fat 5.73g	**29%**
Cholesterol 54.51mg	**18%**
Sodium 219.02mg	**9%**
Potassium 237.91mg	**7%**
Total Carbohydrates 23.57g	**8%**
Fiber 2g	**8%**
Sugar 2.85g	
Protein 5.72g	**11%**

Index

References

[i] Chen M, Bergman RN, Porte D Jr. Insulin resistance and b-cell dysfunction in aging: the importance of dietary carbohydrate. *J Clin Endocrinol Metab,* 1988, *67,* 951-957.

[ii] As cited in Baumel, S. *Dealing with depression naturally.* Lincolnwood Illinois: Keats Publishing. 2000

[iii] O'Keefe SJD, Marks V. Lunchtime gin and tonic: a cause of reactive hypoglycaemia. *Lancet,* 1977, *i,* 1286-1288.

[iv] Fabrykant M, Pacella BL. The association of spontaneous hypoglycemia with hypocalcemia and electro-cerebral dysfunction. *Proc Am Diab Assoc,* 1947, *7,* 233-236

[v] Christensen, L. et. al. Dietary alteration of somatic symptoms and regional brain electrical activity. *Biological Psychiatry.* 29 (7). 1991. Pp. 679-682

[vi] Baumel, S. *Dealing with depression naturally.* Lincolnwood, Illinois: Keats Publishing. 2000

[vii] Airola, P. *Hypoglycemia: A better approach.* Phoenix, Arizona: Health Plus Publishers, 1977.

[viii] Lefèbvre PJ. Hypoglycemia: post-prandial or reactive. *Current therapy in Endocrinology and Metabolism,* 1988, *3,* 339-341, and Lefèbvre PJ. Hypoglycemia or non-hypoglycemia. *Acta Clinica Belgica,*

[ix] As advocated by JF Brun, ibid.

[x] Malaisse, W. et. al. Effects of Artificial Sweeteners on Insulin Release and Cationic Fluxes in Rat Pancreatic Islets. Laboratory of Experimental Medicine, Brussels Free University, 808 Route de Lennik, B-1070 Brussels, Belgium

[xi] Brun, JF ibid

[xii] Duyff, R.American Dietetic Association complete food and nutrition guide. Hoboken, NJ: Wiley & Sons. 2006.

Made in the USA
Middletown, DE
21 October 2014